The Involved School Librarian

School librarians are often in a tricky position because they bear the brunt of political movements but also play a key role in the wider school community. Experienced librarian Hilda K. Weisburg offers a practical approach to help all librarians get more involved while overcoming resistance.

Weisburg unveils the 5 Cs (Confident, Committed, Connected, Communicator, Change Agent), 5 Ps (Passionate, Purposeful, Planner, Professional, Powerful), and 3 Ls (Listener, Learner, Leader) that will help you on your journey. Part I describes how you can recognize your own skills in these areas. Part II has you apply these qualities to improve your interactions with students, teachers, and administrators. And Part III has you apply these concepts to your interactions with the wider community – parents, the library community, and the business community. Each Part ends with a reflection chapter using the four Domains of AASL's National School Library Standards: Think, Share, Create, and Grow.

Both new and experienced school librarians and media specialists will gain valuable ideas for strengthening their programs at a time when school libraries, librarians, and the value they bring are under attack.

Hilda K. Weisburg, MLS, is an author, speaker, and adjunct instructor at William Paterson University (NJ). During her 30+ year career as a school librarian, she served as president of NJASL, volunteered for and chaired several ALA and AASL committees, and received the 2016 AASL Distinguished Service Award. Hilda has written 20 books for school librarians and a young adult novel. On her website, HildaKWeisburg.com, she has a weekly blog on Advocacy and Leadership for school librarians and she runs the School Librarians Workshop Facebook group where well over 17,000 librarians find support.

"*The Involved School Librarian* offers readers at any experience level new methods to improve their performance as school librarians. The 5 Cs (Confident, Committed, Connected, Communicator, Change agent) combined with the 5 Ps (Passionate, Purposeful, Planner, Professional, Powerful) and the 3 Ls (Listener, Learner, Leader) are tools that school librarians can use to work with students, administrators, parents and the broader library community to develop a strong school library program with high levels of support from all constituencies. Part I focuses on the School Librarian, Part II on the campus community, and Part III on the outside community – all using the Cs, Ps and Ls. The writing is clear and straightforward with minimal jargon. Each Part concludes with a Reflection opportunity that supports readers to better implement what they learn through the lenses of Think, Create, Share, Grow, the four domains of AASL's *National School Library Standards for Learners. School Librarians and School Libraries.* This repeated reference to the AASL National Library Standards ensures that readers will be well grounded in these national guidelines as they develop their library practice. This title will be useful to school librarians just beginning their careers, as well as to those further along but looking for new insights to build their skills."

Dorcas Hand, *Co-Chair of Students Need Libraries in Houston ISD grassroots advocacy; Chair, AL Ecosystem Initiative Task Group (2016–2018); Chair, ALA COLA Ecosystem Subcommittee (2023–2026); lead author,* Strengthening Library Ecosystems: Collaborating for Advocacy & Impact *(ALA, 2024), retired school librarian of 40 years*

"Hilda Weisburg is an anomaly. She lives up to the first syllable of her last name—Hilda is wise, knowledgeable, and observes all. But she is also practical and shares the insights she has developed through her expertise and experience with all who will listen. I have recommended her books, some written with Ruth Toor, to both library graduate students and to experienced school librarian practitioners. This book is of particular interest to me because of the two recent books I have co-authored on branding and perception and on library ecosystems. What a companion book to both books this one will be! The book *Elevating the School Library, Positive Perceptions through Brand Behavior* (ALA, 2024) with Susan D. Ballard describes living up to the perceptions of your brand that the school community—faculty, staff, administrators, parents, the business community—have of the school library. And that includes perceptions of you as a leader. After many years working on the ALA Committee on Library Advocacy's Ecosystem Subcommittee and co-authoring *Strengthening Library Ecosystems: Collaborate for Advocacy and Impact* (ALA, 2024) with Dorcas Hand, Michelle Robertson, and Eryn Duffee, I am quite aware that it takes confidence and communication skills to be a leader who will put themselves into a partnership with librarians from other types of libraries to work together, develop a targeted agenda, and take action for legislation and advocacy. Since many school librarians truly are introverts and others lack self-confidence with the attacks hurled in their directions, this book takes a good librarian to the level of a great librarian (thank you, Jim Collins) when someone takes the steps to reflect and then develop a personal plan to increase leadership. This generation of students need those library leaders to teach them critical skills and to support them as they learn. Positive perceptions and increased impact are ahead for those who read this book and make their personal plan!"

Sara Kelly Johns, *Adjunct instructor, Syracuse University iSchool, School Library Program*

The Involved School Librarian

How to Increase Your Impact and Thrive

Hilda K. Weisburg

NEW YORK AND LONDON

Designed cover image: Getty Images

First published 2026
by Routledge
605 Third Avenue, New York, NY 10158

and by Routledge
4 Park Square, Milton Park, Abingdon, Oxon, OX14 4RN

Routledge is an imprint of the Taylor & Francis Group, an informa business

© 2026 Hilda K. Weisburg

The right of Hilda K. Weisburg to be identified as author of this work has been asserted in accordance with sections 77 and 78 of the Copyright, Designs and Patents Act 1988.

All rights reserved. No part of this book may be reprinted or reproduced or utilised in any form or by any electronic, mechanical, or other means, now known or hereafter invented, including photocopying and recording, or in any information storage or retrieval system, without permission in writing from the publishers.

For Product Safety Concerns and Information please contact our EU representative GPSR@taylorandfrancis.com. Taylor & Francis Verlag GmbH, Kaufingerstraße 24, 80331 München, Germany.

Trademark notice: Product or corporate names may be trademarks or registered trademarks, and are used only for identification and explanation without intent to infringe.

Library of Congress Cataloging-in-Publication Data
Names: Weisburg, Hilda K., 1942- author
Title: The involved school librarian : how to increase your impact and thrive / Hilda Weisburg.
Description: New York, NY : Routledge, 2026. | Includes bibliographical references.
Identifiers: LCCN 2025038803 (print) | LCCN 2025038804 (ebook) | ISBN 9781041088103 hardback | ISBN 9781041088080 paperback | ISBN 9781003647058 ebook
Subjects: LCSH: School librarians--United States | Library science--Vocational guidance--United States | School librarian-student relationships--United States | School librarians--Professional relationships--United States | School librarian participation in curriculum planning--United States | Libraries and community--United States
Classification: LCC Z682.4.S34 W448 2026 (print) | LCC Z682.4.S34 (ebook)
LC record available at https://lccn.loc.gov/2025038803
LC ebook record available at https://lccn.loc.gov/2025038804

ISBN: 978-1-041-08810-3 (hbk)
ISBN: 978-1-041-08808-0 (pbk)
ISBN: 978-1-003-64705-8 (ebk)

DOI: 10.4324/9781003647058

Typeset in Palatino
by KnowledgeWorks Global Ltd.

Contents

Meet the Author ix
Foreword x

Introduction 1

Part I: Involving Yourself 5

  1 5 Cs and You 7

  2 5 Ps and You 23

  3 3 Ls and You 40

  4 Reflect on Yourself 57

Part II: Involving Students, Teachers,
Administrators 61

  5 The 5 Cs in Action 63

  6 The 5 Ps in Action 81

  7 The 3 Ls in Action 97

  8 Reflect on Your Involvement with the
     School Community 106

Part III: Involving the Larger Community 109

  9 The 5 Cs in Action 111

10 The 5 Ps in Action........................130

11 The 3 Ls in Action........................143

12 Reflect on Your Involvement with the Wider Community........................155

Meet the Author

 Hilda K. Weisburg has been an Involved School Librarian for over 35 years with excellent communication and organizational skills. She is an active member of the American Library Association (ALA), the American Association of School Librarians (AASL), and the New Jersey Association of School Librarians (NJASL), having served in leadership positions and on committees for her entire career.

Her experience in school and public libraries ranges from preschool through high school. She has been a keynoter and workshop presenter in NJ schools and at state and national conferences. She is currently an adjunct for William Paterson (NJ) U and has been an adjunct for Montana State and also created an online course on Classroom Management for School Librarians based on her book by the same title.

Hilda has written 20 books, co-authoring the early ones with Ruth Toor, and written a well-reviewed YA Fantasy which was a finalist in the International Book Award for Fiction/Fantasy. She also writes a weekly blog on advocacy and leadership for school librarians at https://hildakweisburg.com/blog/ and has a Facebook group for school librarians at www.facebook.com/groups/57409801076.

Foreword

I'll never forget one afternoon in our library. A student came in anxiously holding an assignment. She looked at me and said, "I can't do this." Just flat-out defeat. So we sat down. I didn't give her a lecture or some magic answer. We opened a database. We pulled a couple of books off the shelf. We just started exploring. Slowly, she started asking questions and getting curious. By the time she walked out, she wasn't saying "I can't" anymore. That's what this work is about. That's the heartbeat of a school library.

And honestly, that's also what Hilda K. Weisburg has been reminding us of for decades. That libraries are about possibility, not just information. We're not only shelving books or answering questions—we're helping people believe they can figure things out. We're shaping how kids see themselves. We're giving teachers and administrators a partner. And we're giving communities a center of gravity. Hilda has always understood that, and she's been showing the rest of us how to live it.

If you've ever read *Being Indispensable*, *New on the Job*, *The School Librarian's Career Planner*, or *Leading for School Librarians*, you know what I mean. These aren't "read it once and toss it aside" books. They're the kind you keep nearby. They end up with dog-eared pages and sticky notes because you know you'll need them again.

For me, Hilda has never been just a colleague. She's been a mentor. She's been a friend. She's the kind of person who will stand with you when you're unsure, but also give you that little push when you need to remember your own strengths. Her idea of leadership isn't about titles or awards. It's about showing up, taking action, and believing that even small steps matter. You see it in everyday moments—helping a student find their footing, planning side by side with a teacher, or making sure your library has a voice when decisions get made. That's leadership.

When I look back on my own career, the things that rise to the surface aren't the awards or the bullet points on my résumé. It's the daily conversations with kids. The moments when collaboration with a teacher actually changed a lesson. The quiet wins that added up to something real. That's where the joy has always been. And Hilda has always had a way of reminding me that those are the moments that count most.

Of course, Hilda's professional record speaks volumes. Thirty-five years editing School Librarian's Workshop. More than a dozen coauthored books with Ruth Toor. Leadership in NJASL, leadership in ALA, and conference sessions all over the country. And then in 2016, the AASL Distinguished Service Award. None of that surprised anyone. It just confirmed what we all already knew: Hilda hasn't only made libraries stronger. She's made librarians stronger.

And now we have *The Involved School Librarian*. This isn't a book you'll read once and shelve. It's one you'll turn back to when you need encouragement, or a clear next step, or just the reminder that you're not doing this alone. What I appreciate about this book is that it's not just inspiration—it's something you can actually use. Hilda talks about the 5 C's, the 5 P's, and the 3 L's. On the page they look like lists. But once you start working with them, they turn into a framework—a way to grow into the kind of librarian who doesn't just serve a school, but helps lead it.

The book is built around that growth. First, it asks us to look inward—who we are, how we carry ourselves, what we bring to the table. Then it moves outward—to our daily circle of students, teachers, and administrators. Finally, it pushes us even further out into the community: families, public libraries, local organizations. That's what it means to be involved. It's not about the four walls of the library. It's about being part of the wider circle of learning.

What I love most is the way Hilda reframes challenges. She calls them "Chopportunities." That simple shift—seeing the opening instead of just the obstacle—changes everything. She takes the routine parts of our job—lesson planning, hosting an author visit, fighting for the budget—and ties them back to the bigger mission of equity and access. It's not just theory. It's practical. It's something you can carry with you into school on Monday.

The Involved School Librarian is Hilda's latest gift. It invites us to step into leadership, in small ways and big ones. It reminds us that the work we do every single day really does matter. And it leaves us with this truth, the one Hilda has been teaching all along: the confidence, persistence, and leadership we need aren't out there somewhere. They're already inside us.

Kristina A. Holzweiss
2015 School Library Journal Librarian of the Year

Introduction

In 1931, S. R. Ranganathan published *The Five Laws of Library Science*.[1] Nearly 100 years later the laws are still true. They are as fundamental to libraries today as they were then. The fifth law, "The Library is a growing organism," is the central purpose of *The Involved School Librarian*.

In saying that the library is a growing organism, Ranganathan addressed a basic truth. If an organism is not growing, it is dying. We are all aware that in far too many places, librarians are disappearing, and libraries are dying. What can you as an individual librarian do to prevent this happening to you and your library?

You are doing a good job under stressful conditions. The research shows your value and worth. Yet, those who control your future have not gotten the message.

The Involved School Librarian gives you specific directions on how to reverse this trend. Chapter by chapter, part by part, you create the path that will put you firmly in the minds of all stakeholders. Each chapter progresses, building interlinked connections. As you assimilate one, you use it to easily incorporate the next one. Each reinforces the other. The sections do the same.

The ultimate result is that you become so involved with your many communities that it would be unthinkable to remove you or your library. It sounds like an overwhelming task, but it is broken down into small, easy-to-grasp concepts based on the letters C, P, and L.

Part I focuses on you, because you must be fully cognizant of the strengths you have and those you don't so that you will be able to use them in your daily life.

The 5 Cs are the first ones to incorporate into your strategy for ensuring that your library is a growing organism. Step by step you will discover how to build and use being *Confident*, examine how, why, and where you are *Committed*, explore they ways you need to be *Connected*, identify your needs and abilities to be a skilled *Communicator*, and recognize how to be the *Change Agent* necessary to ensure the library continues to grow.

The 5 Ps are next. To become fully involved you must be *Passionate* in your interactions, *Purposeful* in keeping your focus, a *Planner* to ensure you will reach your goals, *Professional* in dealings with everyone, know you are *Powerful* and how to use that to make the greatest impact.

The 3 Ls complete the letters central to the book's structure. You need to continually polish your skills as a *Listener*, *Learner*, and *Leader*. *Listeners* pay attention. You cannot be Involved with others unless you are fully cognizant of their needs and wants. You, as well as your library, must be a growing organism, which means you are a lifelong *Learner*. Pulling all you have learned about the 5 Cs, 5 Ps, and these 3 Ls, you are the *Leader* who sets the direction for the libraries' ongoing growth. While doing so you are carrying out the Vision of the American Association of School Librarians (AASL) – "Every school librarian is a leader; every learner has a school librarian."

After assimilating the components of being an *Involved School Librarian*, pause and use the four domains of AASL's National School Library Standards[2] – *Think*, *Create*, *Share*, and *Grow* – to reflect on what you have learned about yourself. Who you are now? What needs to change?

Part II moves to the community with whom you interact every day – your students, the teachers, and your administrators.

Now that you understand what goes into being an *Involved School Librarian*, you are ready to apply this understanding to your immediate community. They are the first with whom you need to be involved.

You see students all the time. Most come to the library as part of a class. Others drop in to return or borrow a book, avoid the lunchroom, or possibly be sent to the library to temporarily remove them from the class. You see students as you and they walk through the halls. Depending on the situation and previous contacts, you interact with all of them to some extent. Using the 5 Cs, 5 Ps, and 3 Ls, you become more involved with them, making a positive difference in their lives.

Teachers are your colleagues and friends. Some habitually work with you cooperatively or collaboratively. Others are less inclined to do so. You need to use the 5 Cs, 5 Ps, and 3 Ls to become involved with their practice, becoming a trusted resource and an invaluable help. The goal is for them to find you essential to their teaching and additionally their guide to learning and embracing the newest in tech tools.

Principals and other *administrators* must become more than just evaluators of the library program. Using the 5 Cs, 5 Ps, and 3 Ls, you take the initiative, keeping them informed of trends in technology and sometimes the business world making them look good to their superiors. By knowing their wants and needs, you help them achieve their goals, resulting in you getting your goal of having them recognize that the school library and you are intrinsic to the achievements of the whole school.

Part II concludes as did Part I with a reflection. Use the four domains of AASL's National School Library Standards – *Think, Create, Share,* and *Grow* – to assess your impact on students, teachers, and administrators. What is needed to increase it? How will you do it? Where do you want to go from here?

Part III expands your abilities further outwards into the community including parents, the library community, and the business community. Librarians who have overlooked this last part have been severely hit by the impact this area can have on the continued existence and growth of the library. Although you deal with them infrequently, parents, the library community, including the public library, and local businesses and the people who work there can have a huge impact on the library and you. What they believe the library is and what it does may bear no relation to the reality. It may be based on their memories of their childhood library or what the news is saying about librarians.

Drawing on the 5 Cs, 5 Ps, and 3 Ls, you seek and develop interactions with them. Small exchanges plant seeds. Keeping your goal of the library being viewed as intrinsic to the well-being of students and vital to sustain, you find ways to make the presence of the library and what it achieves into their mental and emotional picture of today's vibrant school library.

As with the other parts, Part III concludes with a reflection using *Think*, *Create*, *Share*, and *Grow*. How well are you building advocates? How can you extend your reach? Are there other sectors of the community you need to explore?

A Summary brings *The Involved School Librarian* to a close. Hopefully you have been using the 5 Cs, 5 Ps, and 3 Ls as you have gone through the book. You are on your way to being a fully Involved School Librarian.

References

1. Ranganathan, S. R. (1931) *Shiyali Ramamrita. The Five Laws of Library Science*; Edward Goldston, Ltd.: London.
2. AASL (2018) *National School Library Standards For Learners, School Librarians, and School Libraries*; ALA Editions: Chicago, Ill.

Part I
Involving Yourself

Socrates said, "To know thyself is the beginning of wisdom." Working from that principle, your journey into becoming a fully *Involved School Librarian* begins with an internal exploration. You are the sum of many parts, experiences, knowledge, and emotions. All have made you into the person you are.

In Part I, we will unpack those parts, doing it through the lens of the 5 Cs, 5 Ps, and 3 Ls. How you see yourself is reflected in the way you deal with others. By looking at the attributes of each of these letters, you will identify the strengths you have and learn how to increase the areas in which you are weaker.

Our minds are powerful. What we believe about ourselves, often unconsciously, can be a barrier to our success. In Part I, you will develop a more positive mindset about how you manifest the attributes that constitute each of the three letters.

So turn the page and let the journey begin.

1

5 Cs and You

Being a school librarian is a challenging, complex, multi-faceted job. You have the necessary training and skills to do it. You work hard at being your best every day. Yet so much of your work is unrecognized, resulting in the perception that you and your library are not invaluable.

It is time to change that perception. Reach those who do not recognize your worth through the interlocking concepts of the 5 Cs, 5 Ps, and 3 Ls. Going letter by letter you enlarge your ability to cause the shift needed in the perception of others to occur.

The beginning starts with you. You also need to make shifts.

Confident

The first of the 5 Cs is *Confident*. How confident are you? You may see yourself as one who is knowledgeable about how to do the job of a school librarian, but you may not be as secure in promoting it. The idea sounds too much like bragging.

We tend to mentally belittle ourselves. We see other librarians as having more talents and skills than we do. While we may only say it inwardly, our inner voice becomes manifested in our body language and daily interactions. We stick to the tried and true rather than risking failure.

The avoidance of risk is common, but that mindset won't help you become involved and interwoven in all your communities.

DOI: 10.4324/9781003647058-3

Others have gotten past it and so can you. Look at the rewards that come with success. Life is full of risk and rewards, and the rewards that come when you are confident enough to step out of your comfort zone are worth it. As with anything you start, the first step is the most difficult.

In a blog post I wrote about "Developing Confidence,"[1] I quoted these ten steps given by Frank Sonnenberg on how to become confident, giving my ideas on how to implement them:

- **Successful Track Record** – Sonnenberg starts with something simple – every win can boost your confidence – no matter the size. If you have trouble recalling these, consider a Success Journal or Win Folder on your computer or on paper so you don't forget your accomplishments. And take a little time to celebrate and cheer yourself. I keep a Success Journal and write in it every day. It not only strengthens my confidence, but it also improves my mindset.
- **Courageous Action** – Look for ways – big and small – to step out of your comfort zone. It can be intimidating but being fearful of failure will keep you from any substantive changes and give you the results you want. Take those first steps (and then add that win to your Success Journal).
- **Prepare and Practice** – Athletes don't just walk out into the field and turn in an outstanding performance. They practice. If you are giving a presentation, write it out, tweak it, tweak it again. If it helps you, learn it almost by heart. For a big project, outline the steps. Create a timeline. Be prepared to adjust that as the project progresses. Nothing is perfect the first time. The more you do, the better you will get.
- **Self-improvement Efforts** – We are lifelong learners. Be committed to your own growth and improvement. Since it's rare for the Professional Development offered by your district to focus on librarian needs, seek out your own PD. Or you can use your Professional Learning Network (PLN), find a mentor, or attend library conferences.

Record the connections and learnings in your Success Journal.
- **Mindset and Attitude** – "If you think you can, or you think you can't, you are right." Our brains are powerful. Don't let yours defeat you. You have been successful before (you have proof!) and will be again. Use your failures as learning opportunities to take into your new endeavor. We teach our students that failing is not failure, quitting is. We must embrace that message for ourselves.
- **Supportive Environment** – Every school has people who see only the negatives. While you must have a collegial relationship with them since the library is for everyone, you don't need to take in their gloomy view of everything. Be closer to people who can see what is good and enjoy what they do. Positive people make it easier to have a confident mindset.
- **Encouraging Comments** – Savor positive feedback. Knowing that others see your achievements is validation. It helps to power you forward. When someone gives you positive feedback, add it to the Win Folder. Record it. Be mindful of how it made you feel and do the same for others. Look for opportunities to give positive feedback to people. Their pleasure will build your own confidence.
- **Self-reflection** – Make time at the end of the day, perhaps on your commute home, to reflect on what you accomplished. Was there a student whose eyes lit up as you helped them find the "just right" book? Did you strike something off your to-do list that you had been putting off? Focusing on these large and small achievements improves self-confidence. (Yup – Success Journal time!)
- **Goal Setting and Achievement** – Getting out of your comfort zone is easier when you make it a goal. Write the goal and develop the action steps needed to attain it. Include a timeline and an assessment. Keep your action steps doable with realistic timelines for achieving them. Record each step you accomplish in your Success Journal. Tweak as you go along. Good news – you can do it again. And of course, Prepare and Practice. With each goal you

achieve, your confidence builds. It becomes easier to tackle a bigger goal. After all, you have a list of successes to prove you can do it.

- ♦ **Personal Values and Beliefs** – This is what holds you steady. *Confidence* comes from within as do your values and beliefs. Consider your "why." Why did you choose to be a librarian? Why do you feel librarians are important? Record your Why on the "title page" of your Success Journal. In addition to our personal values and beliefs, as librarians we hold to the American Library Association (ALA)'s Code of Ethics (www.ala.org/tools/ethics) and the Library Bill of Rights (www.ala.org/advocacy/intfreedom/librarybill). As school librarians we consider AASL's Common Beliefs (https://standards.aasl.org/wp-content/uploads/2017/11/AASL-Standards-Framework-for-Learners-pamphlet.pdf) intrinsic to our program. Build your confidence on your values and you'll see some amazing results.

Committed

With your Success Journal well begun, you are ready to recognize how the next C, being *Committed*, will lead you further into becoming the fully Involved Librarian and make a significant impact on your communities.

Committed is a big word. It means you put your "all" into achieving what you value. You have identified this in the last section of Confidence. The *Cambridge Dictionary* defines it as "loyal and willing to give your time and energy to something you believe in."[2] What are you committed to as a school librarian?

Your commitment comes from your professional and personal "Why." You may want to bring the joy of reading to students, giving them a source of lifetime pleasure and information. Perhaps it has to do with making a difference in students' lives, so they become the critical thinking adults capable of navigating through an ever-increasing information overload, filled with misinformation and other minefields.

Your Why guides you in creating your Mission Statement, which at its core is a pledge proclaiming your commitment to yourself and all who access the library. It is always written in the present tense and brief enough to be remembered and memorized. Fifty words is the outside limit. Your Mission should be on your webpage and posted in the library where it is visible on entry.

I often refer to Mission Statements as your perspiration and your motivation. It is what you do – because of your "Why." As much as possible you want to ensure that whatever task you are involved in connects to your Mission. In crafting it, make sure it aligns with your school and district mission.

Keeping your Mission visible is a constant reminder which we all sometimes need on those very tough, stressful days. It helps to ground you at those times, keeping you on course. Use it in setting priorities and in doing small scale strategic planning.

Your Mission, so publicly displayed, informs others of what you do. It avoids jargon so it is clearly understandable to all. Students view it and may not think much about it, but the more they enter the library, the more it gets filed in their brains. Teachers see it, and you can refer to it when you work with them on developing a learning assignment. Principals and any of their guests notice it when they come into the library. It can be the basis of any conversation you have with them.

Here are two sample Mission Statements:

> The mission of the Blank School Library is to provide students with the opportunity to become lifelong users and creators of information. The library strengthens the curriculum by collaborating with teachers, developing a collection representative of the community, and implementing literacy instruction for students.
>
> The Mission of the Blank School Media Center Program is to create lifelong learners with critical thinking skills, and an appreciation of literature by providing opportunities for all students to gain the self-confidence needed to successfully learn in an information-rich world.

The Mission of the American Association of School Librarians (AASL) is a great example of a powerful, simply written statement. "The American Association of School Librarians empowers leaders to transform teaching and learning."[3] It is only seven words, yet it is a powerful statement proclaiming the organization's commitment to the profession.

Take five minutes before beginning your day by reviewing your Commitment and your Mission. You can do it during your commute. What is on your schedule? How will you bring your commitment to these tasks and activities.

The review is calming and focusing.

Connected

Bring your confidence and commitment to the next C – *Connected*. To be involved, you must be connected. With whom do you need to connect? How do you do it?

Two big questions. Tackling the second one first, the answer is you start small and move outwards. This leads to the answer to the first question. Consider the success of the giant redwood trees. They stand tall and proud in the forest. Yet they have shallow roots. How does something that tall manage to survive strong winds when its roots are shallow? It does so by connecting to the roots of other redwood trees.

Redwood trees have long exemplified "we are stronger together." Starting small, bring that message into all your interactions, beginning with your colleagues. You have friends who are librarians. Reach out to them and encourage them to reach out to you. Interconnect your roots.

If you haven't done so already, stop by the public library. Depending on whether you are an elementary, middle, or high school librarian, introduce yourself to the Children's or Young Adult. Talk about the students who come into the library. What are they looking for? Leisure reading? School assignments? In the course of your conversation, learn how proficient the librarians think the students are, their strengths and weaknesses.

Continue widening your connection into building and expanding a Professional Learning Network (PLN). You all have common experiences in your day. You all deal with similar stresses as well as successes. Your PLN understands those stresses and is there to suggest ways of coping and mitigating them. Your successes and achievements empower them. This is a sustaining connection that will keep you on course, remaining *Confident* and *Committed* to what you do.

Go further into making connections by drawing on your state's school library association. Your membership is imperative. As with the redwoods, they need you to survive, and you need them for the same reason.

Explore the AASL website. What is its Mission and Vision? Can you see how that supports you in your daily work? What resources do they offer? See if they have webinars you can attend. Even if you missed one, they are sometimes available for review. They might have a mentoring program that can help you.

Who are the officers and where do they work? Do you have any personal connection with any of them? You can include them in your growing PLN. Review the list of committees. Do any of them resonate with your interests or areas of concern? Contact the chair to find out if you can be of assistance.

In becoming more involved in your state association, your confidence grows. Your commitment strengthens. Eventually, you may choose to run for an office.

As a *Professional* (see Chapter 2), you should be a member of your state's school library association. It may exist by itself or be a division of the larger association. It undoubtedly has a Facebook and/or a BlueSky page. Use it to ask questions you have and offer solutions to others when you can help. Your connections will continue to grow.

With your state association as part of your PLN, continue expanding outward. Go to the website of the AASL (www.ala.org/aasl). It is the only national association exclusively for school librarians. Explore the tabs to see the many resources it offers you. As a member you will get their journal, *Knowledge Quest*. When reading the articles, note who wrote them. Are there any names you know?

When an article strikes close to home, send an email. The bio of the author at the end of the article will usually give their workplace. That will lead you to their professional email account for you.

Knowledge Quest has a blog which has new posts written by practicing school librarians. The AASL website features links to current ones on its home page. Include reading these brief posts of successful strategies. Some of the authors may become part of your growing PLN.

You can get more specific help on ALA's eLearning page (https://elearning.ala.org/). Search on AASL for a host of webinars that fit your needs on your schedule. Some are free, others have a small fee.

In addition to ALA and AASL, there are two other national organizations that include school librarians. The International Society for Technology in Education (ISTE – https://iste.org/) is your link to the tech people in your school. For many reasons this is a vital connection, as much of your work includes technology, and you want to form a collegial relationship with the department.

Explore their website. Note their Vision on the home page, "Dream Big. Transform Teaching. Empower Learning." Their recently published "Transformation Learning Principles" is available as a free download. The tabs will lead you to more resources, including their standards for students, educators, education leaders, and coaches.

As with ISTE, the Association for Educational Communications & Technology (AECT) is connected to the technology sector of your school. On their home page you can find links to connect you to the broad field that is its focus. It includes opportunities for conversations and signing up for webinars.

Check the Facebook pages of different state school library associations. You often can find additional information and help there. One more way to expand your PLN.

Library Media Network (LM_NET – www.lm-net.info/) was probably the original Facebook group for school librarians connecting librarians around the world. It still functions that way, although many other groups, including my School Librarians Workshop (www.facebook.com/groups/57409801076), have many more members.

Just as you reached out to your local public library, look into the Association for Library Services to Children (ALSC – www.ala.org/alsc) if you work with elementary students or the Young Adult Library Services Association (YALSA – www.ala.org/yalsa) if you are at the high school level. Both associations are part of the Public Library Association which is a division of ALA. (Note that ALSC and YALSA are about to merge.) Each has similar types of resources focused on meeting the needs of the level they serve. Since you work with students of the same age, these divisions offer you more information you can use.

In addition to the tabs on the ALSC home page, scroll down to see the Quick Resource links. Among the Toolkits listed, the Early Trauma Toolkit and the Intellectual Freedom Programming Toolkit connect to your daily practice. Check out ALSC's Blog and Booklists for more ideas.

On the YALSA home page be sure to click on the Advocacy & Issues tab. Explore Advocacy & Activism for ideas on promoting your library and program. Among the Issues & Current Projects, "Putting Teens First" provides resources you can use in your library.

With your knowledge base expanding, your confidence grows. Each of these connections have Mission and Vision Statements aligned with your personal and professional values. Incorporating them into your thinking strengthens your commitment.

While exploring the websites of AASL, ALSC, and YALSA, look for their awards and grants. It takes time to submit a proposal, and you will develop a better focus on what you do and where you want to go in the process. Should you win one, you have additional financial resources to strengthen your program. The association sponsoring the award or grant will publicize it in your community and inform the administration, increasing your impact and showcasing your value.

Focusing on the public libraries is your next outreach. You have already made the connection to the Children and/or Youth Services Librarian in your public library. Widen the relation by looking at your state's Public Library Association and the national one.

The Public Library Association encompasses many aspects of librarianship outside your focus, but still has some noteworthy resources for you. Under PLA Professional Tools, the Technology link has resources on Makerspaces which will guide you in developing or expanding yours. Perhaps you can get a grant to fund a substantial one. Online Learning has both Live and On-Demand Webinars for free and fee. Scroll down to the list of "On-Demand Webinars by Topic" to find those meeting your current needs.

Extend your roots in one more way by seeing what your state teachers' association has to offer. In most states you pay dues to some such organization. The most common one are the state associations connected to the National Education Association (NEA – www.nea.org/). When exploring its home page, look at the Professional Excellence link. It includes information on obtaining micro-credentials which give you the opportunity to choose or create your own professional development. Among the 175+ offered by NEA, you might want to choose from Assessment Literacy and/or Classroom Management.

The American Federation of Teachers (AFT – www.aft.org/) is the association commonly found in states that have strong teacher unions. Focus on PreK-12 Public Education with its link to Schoolhouse Voices featuring short readings on topics of interest. For example, you might look at "Tomorrow's voters must embrace civic responsibility."

You don't want to do all the avenues discussed in anything resembling a short space of time. You needn't do them all. Pick and choose the ones most relevant to begin. Return when you are looking for more connections.

The redwood trees didn't start out tall. The roots intertwined as they grew. This is a journey, not something you complete in a year.

Communicator

You know what you are *Committed* to and are *Confident* in bringing those values into your everyday practice. It's time to look at your next step. Returning to the tree analogy, this time the tree falls.

And as the saying goes, if a tree falls and no one is there to hear it, does it make a noise?

In our work life, the answer is "no." In fact, it is the silence that causes the tree to fall. If you aren't communicating your value, no one knows you are there. It becomes an easy decision for administrators to cut your budget and eventually eliminate your position.

To be involved requires you to communicate the contributions you can and do make to the school community and the larger outside one as well. Done well, it isn't bragging. It does draw on your confidence and should put your Mission into practice. These are the skills and tools of leadership, and all school librarians need to be leaders.

In 1997, Gary Harzell wrote an article in the November issue of *School Library Journal*, entitled "The Invisible School Librarian."[4] Librarians read the article and didn't see the point. At the elementary level they were part of the specialist schedule which gave teachers prep time. At the high school, everyone knew that staffing included a librarian and library as much as it included a nurse and guidance counselors.

Then came December 2007, and the Great Recession began. Budgets were slashed everywhere. Among the first to be cut were the school librarians. What did they do anyway? At the elementary level, they read books to kids. The teachers could do that. Prep time could be accommodated in other ways. At the high school, aides could take over.

In a short time, school librarians began to vanish. In a *Publishers Weekly* article, "Where Have All the School Librarians Gone?"[5] Shannon Maughan quotes results from "SLIDE – The School Library Investigation – Decline or Evolution?" headed by Debra Kachel and Keith Curry Lance showing that between 2010 and 2019 nearly 20% of full-time school librarian positions were eliminated. Hartzell proved to be a Cassandra. He saw the future, but no one took him seriously.

Rebuilding is a slow process. Getting the word out to administrators about the value of school librarians if they don't have one is not a simple task. To help, in 2019, AASL launched the School Administrator Collaborative as a two-year initiative.[6]

The initiative is ongoing. Every two years five administrators, principals, and superintendents are selected to be on the cohort. The goal is "to deepen the visibility and understanding for leadership of an effective school library where the school librarian provides an inclusive and personalized learning environment, creates equitable access to diverse resources, and transforms teaching and learning for all learners."

While this is a positive step in getting school librarians back, there is much to be done, requiring the work of every school librarian still on the job. As always, the more they are involved in their school community, the more their contributions get recognized.

Communication is the key. Indiana University Indianapolis gives this explanation of what a Communicator is and does:

> Communicators convey their ideas effectively and ethically in oral, written, and visual forms across multiple settings, using face-to-face and mediated channels. Communicators are mindful of themselves and others, observe, read thoughtfully, listen actively, ask questions, create messages with an awareness of diverse audiences, and collaborate with others and across cultures to build relationships.[7]

Communication can be broken down into three basic parts: the sender, the message, and the receiver. It sounds so simple. In practice, there are many ways it fails. The message is of the highest importance and the point of communication. It can be lost or misheard if the receiver doesn't hear it – the tree falling in the woods – or the sender isn't clear in crafting it.

We communicate constantly. Our brains keep talking to us. We use all five senses as we interpret messages from people we see and speak with. The message is filtered through our personal history, including culture, biases, and past experiences.

Most of the time our communications happen smoothly, the sender's message is received as intended by the receiver. We count on that happening, but we need to be aware that sometimes it doesn't. The problem could be with the sender, the message, or the receiver.

You might not have given sufficient thought to what you wanted to say. The message may use terms and phrases not familiar to the receiver. The receiver can be in a rush to go someplace. Obstruction in any of the three parts results in the message not being received or it's garbled, lost in the translation.

As a *Communicator* it is necessary for you to be aware of the possibility of messages being misheard or misunderstood. This is true whether you are the sender or the receiver. When you are the receiver of a message that is of some importance, be sure you heard it correctly. Restate it if you have any doubts or questions.

When the message you are sending has a high level of importance, typically related to funds for the library, you want to craft it in a way that the receiver will recognize the significance of it. To do so we typically focus on the supporting data. We have been told this is the best way to show what we are saying is true.

Data is important. However, relying solely on it to send a clear message of a need is most often ineffective. As any business person can tell you, it's emotions that sell. If you watch an automobile commercial, the narrative will be on the features of the car – the data. But you hear the message because the video is showing the wonderful times people are having – the emotions.

Decisions are made from our emotions. We use logic and data to confirm the decision we have already made. Consider how you make your political choices. How much is based on facts? How much on your emotions?

In creating those important messages and requests, use emotions to carry the data. Show a brief video of students creating a project. Have them explain what they learned. Share evidence of kids' produced work. You might have teachers briefly tell how the experience impacted students' learning afterwards.

Where possible, insert your pitch within the emotional content. You might note that the database students are using will not be available next year because your budget was cut. Finish with a short summary of what you are asking. Conclude by tying it to the principal's vision and goals, such as, "I know how much you care about students developing the skills and dispositions needed to be adults. What I am requesting will go far in achieving it."

With significant requests, you almost always find a way to incorporate students into it. They are the emotional tie that bring the most response. Test results are another element as are school and district goals when you connect to them.

Budgets can be another. When you can show how something the library program offers can save money in other areas, you get heard. For example, the library databases can slow the cycle of replacing textbooks.

Illustrate your message so your audience understands them as clearly as possible. Pictures, graphics, and videos are more quickly internalized than text. Use the language your receivers understand. If you are talking with administrators in schools, they know the educational terms but not library terminology. Make any needed changes to be sure your message isn't garbled.

Check out the "Because Statements" from ALA's Libraries Transform project (https://ilovelibraries.org/librariestransform/toolkit/). Use those that apply as needed. The templates on the site give you the opportunity to add your own. Better yet, have students and/or teachers post their "because" statements.

Communications on core issues require planning. You don't go into a meeting with your principal without doing significant preparation. You are clear about your "ask" – your message. And you craft it in a language that your principal understands. The message show how your "ask" will be a positive impact on their goals.

While interactions with supervisors carry much weight, your everyday communications count as well. The ones with administrators occur infrequently, but you interact every day with the teachers and students. You are always communicating.

Change Agent

The 5th C, being a *Change Agent*, requires you to draw on the other 4 Cs. Making changes carries risk, and risk implies the possibility of failure. You need your confidence to go forward. The reason for the changes you want to make are rooted in your values, and Mission – your commitments. You can't make significant changes without drawing on others, necessitating your connections and your ability as a *Communicator*.

In your life span, you have seen many changes in the library. If you have been in education or libraries for a while, much has occurred. It is almost laughable to see how you used to do your job and what it entailed compared with what you do today.

Ask people what a library is, and their answer will depend on when they were last in a library. To a few who remember it from their childhood, it is a place for books, whether picture books or the reference resources of their high school and college days. Current users know that technology plays a major role in in the library program. But what all of them tend to do is "freeze frame" their mental picture.

What they overlook is that the library needs to be ever-changing. As stated in the Introduction, Ranganathan was correct.[8] The fifth law, "The Library Is a Growing Organism," speaks to libraries always changing to meet the needs of users.

Referring to the library as an organism, Ranganathan expressed another truth. Like all organisms, if it isn't growing, it is dying. There is no stasis in nature. The law and its implication proved prophetic. Those libraries without librarians began withering on the vine. They become frequented less and they disappear. The room is repurposed.

To prevent the further disappearance of libraries, it is necessary to ensure that your library is a growing organism. Be alert to what's next. Connect with your colleagues at the local, state, and national levels. Attend webinars and conferences. Follow the leaders and shakers who have proven track records as change makers.

Make it a practice to know what is happening in the business and tech world. Most of what's next comes from there. When you see something new on the horizon, consider how it would fit in the library. What are the implications for you program? You need to be able to hit the ground running. Many times, you will be responsible for bringing these changes to teachers.

You role as a change agent comes into play in another significant way. As a leader, you have the ability and responsibility to create more leaders. Referring once again to the AASL Vision,

"Every school librarian is a leader; every learner has a school librarian," it is you who has the power to make this vision a reality.

Others have mentored you. Who can you mentor? Look for those new to the field. Even if they have been classroom teachers for years, they are new to librarianship and the many roles they need to play. Encourage them to volunteer for committees in your state library association. Let them know you are there to help.

Every time you help create a leader, you have helped restore libraries to students, teachers, administrators, and those outside as well. It is an ongoing challenge. Employing all 5 Cs will involve you in every aspect of your communities.

References

1. Weisburg, H. K. (2024) *Developing Confidence*; https://hildakweisburg.com/?s=developing+confidence
2. Cambridge English Dictionary (n.d.) *Committed*; https://dictionary.cambridge.org/us/dictionary/english/committed
3. American Association of School Librarians (n.d.) www.ala.org/aasl/about/govern
4. Hartzell, G. N. (1997, November) The invisible school librarian: Why other educators are blind to your value. *School Library Journal*, 43(1): 24–27.
5. Maughan, S. (2021, December 10) Where have all the school librarians gone? *Publishers Weekly*. www.publishersweekly.com/pw/by-topic/industry-news/libraries/article/88111-where-have-all-the-school-librarians-gone.html
6. American Library Association News (2019, May 24) AASL launches school administrator collaborative. www.ala.org/news/2019/05/aasl-launches-school-administrator-collaborative
7. Indiana University Indianapolis (n.d.) Profiles of learning for undergraduate success. https://profiles.indianapolis.iu.edu/profiles/communicator/index.html
8. Librarianship Studies & Information Technology (2022, September 11) Five laws of library science. www.librarianshipstudies.com/2017/09/five-laws-of-library-science.html

2

5 Ps and You

With the 5 Cs in your toolbox, we turn to the 5 Ps: Passionate, Purposeful, Planner, Professional, and Powerful. Like the 5 Cs, the Ps are linked sequentially and backwards, interlocking them, so that you increasingly become fully involved within the communities you serve.

The 5 Ps blend emotions with intentions. Combining the two gives them extra strength to become the driving forces that power you forward. Discover how they can work within you so that you are prepared to employ them in dealing with others.

Passionate

The Britannica Dictionary defines Passion as "a strong feeling of enthusiasm or excitement for something or about doing something."[1] As school librarians we are passionate about what we do. In many ways, it is how we define ourselves. Whether you are a beginner or a long-time practitioner, you are apt to say, "Once a librarian, always a librarian."

The multi-faceted job of a school librarian is inevitably stressful. Because we serve so many on so many levels we can be pulled at from different directions. What keeps us engaged in our daily life is to access the passion we have for what we do.

Your Passion is rooted in your "Why", which you explored in the previous chapter. The Mission you created or tweaked then is the basis for how you do your job. Your Vision, which is your inspiration and aspiration, comes from your strong desire – or passion – to bring that vision into reality. Achieving that seemingly unreachable goal would mean that everything you believe libraries and librarians can be and do would be seen and recognized by all.

Become more aware of the Passion residing within you. Note when it surfaces. It can happen when you make a significant connection with a student. Perhaps a teacher or an administrator makes a positive comment about the library and/or your contribution to it. A negative assessment about the value of the library might equally stir your Passion.

When these instances, however fleeting, occur, take a moment to note them. Be conscious of how your Passion adds dimension to your interactions and practice. Your Passion affects your mindset. In turn, this colors your responses to others.

To be a fully Involved School Librarian, you need to have strong relationships within your communities. Your mindset is a tool to achieving that. People are attracted to those who radiate a positive outlook. It's not being an irrepressible optimist who refuses to see anything wrong. On the contrary, a positive outlook comes from the belief that you and others will find a solution to whatever obstacle is in the path.

Before you can demonstrate a positive mindset, you need to cultivate it within yourself. Look at obstacles and crises as a "Choppportunity." On May 27, 2019, I wrote a blog post, "Crisis? No! It's a Chopportunity"[2] in which I explained I first learned the word at an earlier *School Library Journal* Summit.

The mashup word is a combination of challenge and opportunity. Instead of reacting with anger, alarm, or any other negative reaction to something affecting your job, pause. See it not as a crisis but a challenge to your creativity and find the opportunity it opens.

A small challenge school librarians often face is having the principal inform you that you need to close the library and cover a class. You never say "no" to an administrator, however you can say that you don't want to disappoint teachers by cancelling their scheduled classes, and suggest instead of going to the classroom, the students come to the library. This will give students an extra opportunity to have library time.

See the "Chopportunity?" You haven't complained about being asked (required) to go to the classroom, showing you are a team player. You have let your principal know the library is important to the teachers. You have brought the kids to the library and got an idea of what the teacher is working on. When the teacher returns, you can now offer your help to the teacher or completing the assignment students had.

Even if you don't have a class scheduled in that time block, bringing the students to the library is a plus. Other than showing the principal the importance of the library to the teachers, the other positive results apply. You have turned a mini crisis into a "Chopportunity."

A major crisis might be a budget cut. Just the incentive you need to look for other sources of funds. It's the perfect opportunity for a Go-Fund-Me or DonorsChoose. You might look into grants and awards offered by your state educational association and the American Association of School Librarians (AASL). Perhaps the parent-teacher association would be willing to run a fund raiser.

"Chopportunities" require out-of-the-box thinking, and they require Passion. Without Passion, it's easy to quit. Accept what came down. After all, it's not your fault. And who has time to do the extra work involved? But Passion has you rising to the challenge and finding new and creative ways to grow the library, find new Connections (as discussed in Chapter 1), build awareness of the library's importance, and develop new library supporters and advocates.

Every time you take on a "Chopportunity," your knowledge base increases and so does your Passion for being a school librarian. Success encourages you to be always open for a "Chopportunity." Your mindset is positive as you are *Confident* that you can weather any storms that might come your way. The positive mindset draws people to you, making it easier to build the Connections that make you a fully Involved School Librarian.

Purposeful

Being Purposeful means you bring determination and intention to what you do. Being Purposeful brings emotion to your commitments, and emotions are a driving force. When coupled with your Passion it fuels you in achieving your big and small goals. Some you accomplish daily, others are extended over weeks, months, and even years as your overall purpose is declared in your Mission Statement. Being Purposeful brings emotion to your commitments.

Your smaller goals include the learning outcomes of a lesson for students, whether it's reading with elementary students or a research problem with middle and high school students. You have goals, although you might not write them down as such, when you open a conversation with teachers about a future cooperative or collaborative lesson or initiate a meeting with your principal. In the latter case, it could possibly be the positive result of an email you are sending to set up that meeting. The idea is to be aware of being purposeful as much as possible in all your interactions.

As a Purposeful Librarian, you embrace and demonstrate the six Common Beliefs of AASL's National School Library Standards.[3] As an Involved School Librarian, the educational and even the outside communities recognize the importance and truth of them as well.

Re-look at these six Common Beliefs to identify where you need to make them a reality for your communities:

1. *The school library is a unique and essential part of a learning community* – The goal is for the learning community to recognize that the library is unique and essential. Draw on what you learned about being a Communicator.
2. *Qualified school librarians lead effective school libraries* – Even within the education field, too many are unaware of the specialized training required to become a school librarian and the many roles we have. When you are conscious of being Purposeful, you can casually insert

references to your skills and jobs which are part of your day into conversations you have with teachers, parents, and administrators. If you have volunteers, you can highlight the scope of your activities which they might have witnessed but not given thought to it. Don't overdo this. It should be an occasional thing.

3. *Learners should be prepared for college, career, and life* – While classroom teachers focus on specific skills, following a subject-based curriculum, your focus is broader. Give teachers credit for the foundational skills they bring to students while letting them know how this background has enabled them to discover how their classroom learning, coupled with their library experiences, prepares them for wherever their futures take them.

4. *Reading is the core of personal and academic competency* – The statement is obvious, but it will take purposefulness to show others how essential the library's collection of fiction, nonfiction, and digital resources build the competency while addressing the needs of diverse students, ensuring that all learners see themselves and recognize the worth of others.

5. *Intellectual freedom is every learner's right* – The library collection is the basis for ensuring that freedom. Freedom of speech includes the freedom to read differing opinions. The library must be a safe space for all. Look for ways to communicate to your connections this fundamental concept of libraries.

6. *Information technologies must be appropriately integrated and equitably available* – Assumptions are made that everyone has access to technology. Kids are attached to their screens. Technology is omnipresent in our world. What is overlooked are economic and physical factors that inhibit or block access for a number of students. Home internet access and wi-fi availability costs are beyond the resources of some families. Students with physical disabilities, including vision, hearing, and mobility, can have difficulties in using various aspects of technology. The library actively seeks and acquires the

means to address these barriers. Your skills as a Change Agent make it possible to incorporate the modifications needed so all learners have equitable access. Your ability as a Communicator informs your communities of what has been added to the technology in the library and why it is important.

Pause to review the Mission Statement you created or revised in Chapter 1. To what extent does it address the six Common Beliefs?

In managing the numerous components of your job, check in with yourself to see where you are being Purposeful in handling them. Incorporating all the Cs and Ps, with more letters to come, may seem complex and impossible. It is – at the beginning.

The reality is you won't do it as often as indicated here, but over time, you will become increasingly aware of them. The interconnection of these letters makes it easier to implant them in your mind. One day, you will realize that you are manifesting all of them as they have become the grounding that allows you to be the Involved School Librarian, valued by all your communities.

Planner

Planning is natural to you. It is how you manifest your Mission and Vision. You plan lessons. You plan displays. You plan author visits. You know the basics of planning. Now it's time to upgrade your techniques.

Planning at all levels starts with the desired outcome. It may be the enduring understandings you want students to gain as a result of the lesson. With a display, you might seek to have students become aware of titles and authors they didn't know. An author visit is often used as a motivator to read not only the visiting authors but also to become aware of an author's purpose in writing the book or books and thus to think more critically about their reading.

To improve your planning, revisit your desired outcomes or goals. Do they forward your Mission Statement? To what extent do they take you closer to your Vision?

In developing your Action Plan for achieving the goal, look to your connections. How are you involving the teacher with the lesson you are planning?

Is there someone more creative than you who could help with the display? You could then let others, particularly the principal, know of that person's contribution. Perhaps students could participate in constructing the display. Inform the principal about this as well, drawing on your ability as a Communicator.

How are you going to prepare students for the author visit? Does it connect to your Mission and Vision? Which teachers are you informing about the visit? You need to be a Connector and Communicator to have them not see this as an intrusion on what they are doing with their students. Perhaps together you can see a way to tie it to the lesson they are working on.

Talk to the principal before beginning the process of planning the visit. Be prepared to discuss your desired outcomes to ensure that they see the value of the visit. Alert them to key information including the date and time of the visit and any additional guests you would like to have.

Obviously invite the principal, but you might also want to invite your superintendent. If possible, invite parents. This extends your external community's awareness of the important role of the library and librarian. Take pictures and share the story of the visit on your library website or, even better, on a newsletter you do. Consider asking a reporter from the local press to cover the event.

What will be your funding source for the event? Will you use Donors Choose? How long will it take to raise enough money? Your connection to your PLN should be able to advise you.

Your Action Plan should include a "by when" date for each step and identify who needs to be contacted or involved in that step. Be prepared to adjust it since plans almost never go exactly as anticipated. Again, inform your principal if you make any significant changes. You must never blindside an administrator.

Save all the information related to the event, particularly the reactions of the students after the event and how it achieved your desired outcome. Include this in your end of the year summary of the library activity for your principal.

Strategic Planning

Unlike planning for your day, you must be able to plan and execute a Strategic Plan. It will take your Confidence, as tackling a big job is risky. You need to be Committed because a lot will depend on your carrying the plan to fruition. The plan will get accepted by your administrators more readily because you have established a communication channel with them. Of course, this is an example of how you function as a Change Agent. Your Passion and Purpose guide you throughout.

The Strategic Plan looks similar to the planning you did for the author visit with significant differences. The Action Plan is much longer and will require more tweaking as you go along. The author visit took months, which gives you some idea of what else is needed, but the Strategic Plan is normally for two to three years, and you should always have a Strategic Plan you work on.

Most library strategic planning is for advocacy. Identify your purpose. Who or what is the object of the plan? It could be targeted at reaching your school community or for the larger outside community. I did one for a major library renovation project.

Understand the difference between a strategy and a tactic. Your strategy is tied to your Vision. The tactics are the steps needed to get there. Frank Muir authored the classic explanation of the difference between the two. "Strategy is buying a bottle of wine when you take a lady out to dinner. Tactics is getting her to drink it."[4]

In World War II, the Allies' strategic objective was to remove Japanese strongholds in tiny Pacific islands. The Japanese forces were dug in, and it would cost numerous lives to take the islands one by one. The tactics involved bombing oil supplies, which significantly reduced what were the high casualties of the landing troops.

As a leader, you are a strategist. You hold the long-range objective – the Vision. Managers (which you are as well) carry out the plan as they accomplish the Mission, employing tactics to do so.

The parts of a Strategic Plan are similar in some ways but more comprehensive than a basic lesson plan. Create the outline for it on a spreadsheet, adding more details as you go along.

Start with the strategic objective. What are you trying to accomplish and why? It should take your library closer to achieving your Vision.

For example, your Vision might be: *The vision of our school library media program is for equitable and intellectual access to the school library's information resources and tools required for student success. A safe, open, accessible and inviting learning library commons is essential to student achievement, citizenship and support the principles of intellectual freedom.* Your strategic objective might be to renovate the library to create barrier-free access to library resources while creating a more open space for collaboration and better prepare all students for their future.

The first column of the Action Plan sequentially lists all the necessary steps. In developing your Action Plan, expect to add steps as you learn more about what is required.

The second column explains what needs to be done and by whom. You might divide this so you have a "by whom" for the second column and a "to do" column for the third.

In this case your first step would be to learn what adaptive technologies and physical changes are necessary to address the needs of students and possibly staff disabilities. From learning about changes to your computers to lowering the height of the circulation desk, the alterations will be numerous and costly.

The "by whom" for that step would be you. But there might be others on the staff who are knowledgeable in this area and could be of help.

Include plans to contact companies that address these needs. They will be of help in determining the costs and the time it will take to complete the job. Since your plan is multi-year the costs will be broken down by budget years.

Before you go much further with your steps, speak with your administrators. You want them solidly behind the plan. Bring your strategic objective to the meeting. Be sure to tie it to their goals and vision. The better it fits with their needs and wants the more likely that you will get approval. If possible, share your spreadsheet to show you can carry out the plan.

The fourth column is "by when" it needs to be done. It will keep you on track and is the column that alerts you to when it's necessary to make adjustments.

Don't be afraid of the changes needed. This is a big, multi-year plan. It never goes exactly as originally envisioned. Prepare yourself to make mistakes. They do happen. The few that do will be overshadowed by your success and probably not noticeable to others.

The fifth and final column keeps those mistakes to a minimum. It is for assessments. You want to see to what extent the steps in your plan are bringing the desired result. If they aren't, it is another place where you might need to make adjustments or even add a step. It's an ongoing process.

You are undertaking a big job and need to reduce the stress it causes. One technique I developed and used in doing two major renovations of my libraries is something I call Microscoping, Telescoping, and Periscoping.

In Microscoping you focus on the next steps of your Action Plan with due dates in the immediate future. By not worrying about all that still must be done, you can complete these with full concentration.

Telescoping is for taking the long view. You might do it monthly or even bi-monthly. Recognize how much you have accomplished and look forward to your end goal.

Periscoping should be scheduled weekly, either on Friday or Monday. It's when you pop up your periscope to see what's coming up in the near future. You want to be prepared for it so it doesn't catch you by surprise.

The three together will keep you on track. Due dates might shift. Steps might be added, but you still are headed in the right direction. The date your project is over, which could be somewhat later than you planned, you have successfully achieved the goal of your Strategic Plan. You have taken a giant step to achieving your Vision.

While you work on your Action Plan, you are still busy with lesson plans, creating displays and bulletin boards, and perhaps scheduling an author visit or some other library promotional event. The daily work of the library is ongoing.

In managing all these activities, make time for self-care. You want to be able to enjoy the culmination of your Strategic Plan. Cheer yourself on as you complete a step. Celebrate milestones. Buy yourself a special dessert. Get a massage. You earned it. And plan something special when you welcome everyone to the barrier-free library with a more open space for collaboration.

Your new library has opened the door into the future for your students.

Professional

The word *"Professional"* doesn't seem to carry emotion, and yet in many ways it does. Professional is about your presence. The perception others have about what a librarian is and the academic training required doesn't lend itself to their recognizing you are a Professional.

Being a Professional is communicated in how you present yourself to others. It requires Confidence and is rooted in your Commitment. You are the face of the library, and it's vital that you are seen as a Professional.

Merriam-Webster defines Professional as:

1. "characterize by or conforming to the technical or ethical standards of a profession
2. exhibiting a courteous, conscientious, and generally businesslike manner in the workplace"[5]

Both definitions apply to being a *Professional* as a school librarian. Unlike lawyers who can be disbarred if they violate their ethic, you don't lose your status as a librarian if you don't abide by the ethics of the profession. However, you do lose some of the grounding that helps give you a Professional presence if you don't.

As a school librarian you should be familiar with ALA's Code of Ethics.[6] Review the nine statements that embody the principles of our profession:

1. We provide the highest level of service to all library users through appropriate and usefully organized resources;

equitable service policies; equitable access; and accurate, unbiased, and courteous responses to all requests.
2. We uphold the principles of intellectual freedom and resist all efforts to censor library resources.
3. We protect each library user's right to privacy and confidentiality with respect to information sought or received and resources consulted, borrowed, acquired, or transmitted.
4. We respect intellectual property rights and advocate balance between the interests of information users and rights holders.
5. We treat co-workers and other colleagues with respect, fairness, and good faith, and advocate conditions of employment that safeguard the rights and welfare of all employees of our institutions.
6. We do not advance private interests at the expense of library users, colleagues, or our employing institutions.
7. We distinguish between our personal convictions and professional duties and do not allow our personal beliefs to interfere with fair representation of the aims of our institutions or the provision of access to their information resources.
8. We strive for excellence in the profession by maintaining and enhancing our own knowledge and skills, by encouraging the professional development of co-workers, and by fostering the aspirations of potential members of the profession.
9. We affirm the inherent dignity and rights of every person. We work to recognize and dismantle systemic and individual biases; to confront inequity and oppression; to enhance diversity and inclusion; and to advance racial and social justice in our libraries, communities, profession, and associations through awareness, advocacy, education, collaboration, services, and allocation of resources and spaces.

The Code of Ethics was first adopted by ALA in 1939 and amended four times, the last being June 29, 2021. The statements are a declaration of how we view our chosen profession and how we carry out our many roles and responsibilities. They are not always easy to uphold.

- ♦ There have always been challenges. We are seeing strong attacks on libraries and the principles we endorse. Politics are a big part of the challenges today and have been at times in the past. The question for you is how do you respond to them?
- ♦ The decision is personal and, as noted, you won't lose your library certification if you cave in to powerful forces. But submitting takes away from who you are as a Professional and is damaging to how you see yourself.

Whether it is one parent challenging a book or a large-scale orchestrated assault, lean in on your professional associations. You may be the only librarian in your school, but you are not alone. It is easier to resist when you aren't isolated. Your state school library association, AASL, and ALA have resources to help you. So do ISTE and ASCD (Association for Supervisors and Curriculum Developers).

While your membership in these associations connects you to the resources, as a *Professional* and an Involved School Librarian you need to go further. It is not enough to only pay your annual dues and perhaps attend a conference. It is important for you to be an active member.

Serving on committees and even running for an office takes time but the rewards are many. Your confidence grows. You gain a larger perspective on issues. Your vocabulary changes as you interact with leaders. Their terminology becomes part of yours. As a result your communications are altered.

The small changes in how you address ideas and speak with all your patrons are perceived by them subconsciously. How you carry yourself because of your increased confidence adds to that perception. You are seen as a *Professional*.

Your connections are another resource. You have built relations within and outside your school community. As an Involved School Librarian you have become interwoven in the fabric of their lives. They know your value, your worth, and will be there to support you.

Professional as it applies to school librarians does not apply to dress. When we picture a professional, we tend to think of the power suit of a lawyer or the white coat with a stethoscope of a doctor. Librarians are well past the cardigan of the stereotype. They dress like the other teachers.

Our presence as a *Professional* comes from how we meet and treat our patrons, whether students, teachers, administrators, parents, and any other guests to the library. The library is our home. We work to make it look welcoming and we strive, as our ethics illustrate, to welcome everyone equally. The Passion we have for what we do furthers the sense of feeling welcomed and adds to our being seen as a Professional.

You are developing more ways to become the Involved School Librarian. You have integrated the 5 Cs – Confident, Committed, Connected, Communicator, and Change Agent – along with being Passionate, and Purposeful. Together they build your presence as a *Professional*.

Powerful

It is all too easy to feel powerless. Those you interact with every day feel that way. Students and teachers regularly complain they feel powerless.

The sense of powerlessness may be contagious, but you can't afford to feel or be powerless. Shift your mindset and realize you can be *Powerful* in your communities. An Involved School Librarian exudes a sense of power.

Begin by identifying what power is. It's the ability to cause or create change and the ability to make people do things. The word "make" implies holding a position that can reward or punish people. Focusing on the word "make" fails to describe the different types of power.

In 1959 social psychologists John R. P. French and Bertram Raven identified these five distinct bases of social power:[7] legal, coercive, reward, expert, and referent (charismatic).

Legal Power comes from a title.

Coercive is the power to punish and is paired with Reward Power.

Reward Power is the ability to give you something of value. Combined with Coercive, they form the classic "carrot and stick."

Expert Power is knowing something that another values and/or needs to know.

Referent or *Charismatic Power* is having people do what you want because they like working and being with you.

The last two are your obvious "go-to" choices. You also have the second and third in how you treat requests and deal with teachers and students. Since the library serves everyone, you avoid using these two.

Lisa VeneKlasen and Valeries Miller defined power more simply[8] as Power Over, Power With, Power To, and Power Within.

Power Over is coercive power. Our administrators have it. So do teachers. Some wield it with a hand of steel. The more successful ones use a gentle touch. I had a superintendent who never used threats, direct or implied, and yet principals and teachers quickly fell into line. She used her ability as a Connector and Communicator to know how to frame an "ask" and get the results she wanted.

By contrast, the high school principal at the time used to tell people he was the boss. The staff complied only as specifically directed. The superintendent never told people she was the boss. They knew and did everything they could to help her out and gain her approval.

Power With is finding common ground among different interests and building collective strength. It is based on mutual support, solidarity. It is the basis of relationship building.

Utilize your ability as a *Connector* to identify and strengthen the bonds you have already made. It builds advocacy, recognizing together we are stronger. We have seen the power of individuals working together to make a change. Power With eases the way in your planning as teachers and your administrators get their goals by working with you.

Power To refers to the unique potential of every person to shape his or her life and world. Advocacy efforts incorporate the belief that each individual has the power to make a difference. When you have made the connections and built the relationships, you help others see that what they do, no matter how small, makes a difference.

Power Within is an inner force. It comes from feeling *Confident*. It is a powerful belief in yourself. When you trust yourself, you are better able to utilize Power With, making the library thrive. William Henley exemplified Power Within in the last lines of his poem "Invictus," declaring, "I am the master of my fate: I am the captain of my soul."

When you recognize the different types of power, you discover which ones you have been using and which ones you need to develop further. You have greater strength than you realize. You truly are *Powerful*.

The 5 Ps are linked sequentially. Your passion fuels your purpose which in turn drives your planning. Your plans bring you closer to your Vison which is rooted in your purpose and further your presence as a *Professional*. In combination they make you a *Powerful* leader.

References

1. The Britannica Dictionary (n.d.) *Passion*. Retrieved March 6, 2025, from www.britannica.com/dictionary/passion.
2. Weisburg, H. K. (2019) *Crisis? No! It's a Chopportunity*. https://hildakweisburg.com/2019/05/.
3. AASL (2018) *National School Library Standards For Learners, School Librarians, and School Libraries*; ALA Editions: Chicago, Ill.
4. BrainyQuote (n.d.) *Frank Muir*. Retrieved October 1, 2025, from www.brainyquote.com/quotes/frank_muir_391566.
5. Merriam-Webster Dictionary (n.d.) *Professional*. Retrieved March 17, 2025, from www.merriam-webster.com/dictionary/professional.
6. ALA (American Library Association) (n.d.) *Code of Ethics*. Retrieved March 17, 2025, from www.ala.org/tools/ethics.

7. French, John R. P. and Raven, Bertram H. (1959) The bases of social power. In Cartwright, D. (ed.). *Studies in Social Power*; Ann Arbor, MI: Research Center for Group Dynamics, Institute for Social Research. pp. 150–167.
8. VeneKlasen, L. and Miller, V. (2002) *Power and Empowerment.* PLA Notes. Retrieved October 1, 2025, from www.iied.org/sites/default/files/pdfs/migrate/G01985.pdf (p. 55).

3

3 Ls and You

Building on what you have discovered about the 5 Cs and the 5 Ps, you are ready to incorporate the 3 Ls into your wheelhouse.

Listener

The 3 Ls begin with *Listener.* How would you rate yourself as a Listener? Can you identify the main information the other person imparted? Are you able to spot any sub-text communication that accompanied it?

Being a *Listener* sounds like a passive behavior. However, an Involved School Librarian recognizes it is an active skill. Being a good Listener requires an understanding of what is involved and can require changes in habits.

Multitaskers find it extremely difficult to focus exclusively on what the other person is saying. In failing to do so, they miss the ability to respond in a way that furthers connections, builds relationships, and alerts them to best actions to take in the situation.

You must deal with the simple fact that communication is a constant. It never stops. Our brains are continuously processing all kinds of data. We communicate in words, in text, pictures, art, music, and dance.

Since we are constantly communicating you would think we would all be experts at it. But our communications go off sometimes. And when they do, the results have consequences.

Understanding the elements of communication enables you to communicate more clearly and recognize where the message might have become garbled.

All communication consists of three parts: the sender, the message, and the receiver. The parts are present whether the communication is spoken, written, or silent. A good Listener is adept in all three.

Conversation is like a tennis game. The sender sends the message to the receiver who then becomes the sender when responding with their own message to the original person who is now the receiver. And so, it continues.

It took a lot of words to describe what sometimes happens in seconds. But just as with tennis the ball doesn't always go where it was intended. To prevent the ball from going astray, it is important to discover how to improve your skills as a Listener.

There has been much discussion of what active listening entails. The listener is fully attentive to the speaker or sender. Eye contact is maintained throughout but may include being able to take notes on what was said. The receiver never interrupts the speaker.

When the speaker finishes, the receiver responds by summarizing what was said to confirm understanding. Notes can help with this, but it is better to be able to do this without them. Your ability demonstrates you were fully focused on what they were saying.

The listener's response prevents any misunderstanding and allows for a further interchange. Additionally, it demonstrates your interest in what was said, creating a climate for cooperation. The door is open to further such conversations and is the beginning of building or increasing a relationship.

It is important to remember that having a conversation with those who are on the autism spectrum is different. For example, don't expect an immediate answer to a question you ask. While teachers are informed about kids with special needs, usually you aren't notified. Reach out to the guidance counselor to find out about any students who are neurodivergent and ask for whatever guidance they have given teachers about how to interact with these students.

The second part of communication is the message. It is the purpose of the communication and can be the cause of that ball going in the wrong direction.

Keep the ball on course by being mindful of who the receiver is, what they know and don't know about the subject. Know when to use jargon and when to avoid it.

Using terminology familiar to the listener increases the likelihood of it being heard accurately. The reverse sets up a barrier to a clear message. The message will be misinterpreted in some way.

In attempting to ensure that our message is understood, we can over-explain. Continuing the tennis analogy, if the message is too long or too complex, the receiver might just leave their side of the net. By the time the ball lands, the receiver is gone.

You gave some thought to the receiver's background in creating your message, but communication can fail because of the receiver. You lost the receiver with the long message, but you also can lose the receiver because they didn't come to you for the information. You just interrupted what they were intending to do.

Being a good *Listener* goes beyond what is said. It encompasses the extensive information communicated in body language. Throughout the conversation a stream of body language is occurring.

When we think of body language we usually think of the face. It is the most obvious part of body language in action. Although the face has many parts, it goes far beyond the face. Body language is a basic communication tool whether we are aware of it or not. Animals use it to communicate fear, aggression, and sexual attraction. They bristle, they intimidate, they puff up, they nuzzle, they cower in submission. And in many ways, we do the same.

You meet someone. You immediately identify whether you know the person or not. Whether your connection is positive or negative, you read their body language and make some assessment of what is to come. You respond with your own body language.

Not a word is spoken, but communication has occurred. Usually all of it happens below your conscious recognition. You might think of it when you are approached by someone you don't like or want to talk to but for various reasons you need to be polite.

You usually try to control your expression when that occurs, but that doesn't always work. You need to change your mindset. Your face is a powerful communicator.

Lips speak even when not talking. If they are in action, the first thing we usually notice is the mouth. Are the lips turned up slightly? It's a sign of recognition and pleasure. The breadth of a smile indicates the degree of happiness the person has in seeing you. Usually, you return the message in kind.

The smile is a strong communicator. When it is a true smile, and we can usually tell the difference, it says you see them as a person. You have recognized them as a person you like or want to get to know.

A favorite saying of mine is, "The world is like a mirror. Smile at it, and it will smile back." People respond positively to a friendly face, which makes any interchange go better. This doesn't mean you go around grinning from ear-to-ear. Just having your lips turn up slightly sends out a positive message.

What happens when you smile and don't mean it? How can you tell? Besides becoming an actor, how can you send a smile when you don't mean it? When you see a fake smile, you usually go on alert. Yet we are so conditioned to smile, there are times when you smile and don't mean it.

Emojis have become common because we use our faces to communicate. Take out your phone and turn your camera on. Play with different expressions. See how often your brows and forehead come into play. They telegraph worry and uncertainty. They also express sympathy, concern, and amazement.

What are sometimes called "the 11's" are the two lines above your nose. When you are happy, they are at rest. But when you get angry, they deepen, and your brows come together. Your lips rarely react at all. The message is all in the brow.

Tilt your head to one side. If your face is at rest, the position sends a message that you are listening. When coupled with other facial expressions, the head tilt emphasizes most of them. Use the camera again to see how it affects the intensity of the emotion you are sending.

Your silent communication includes more than your face. Your whole body comes into play. Arms, shoulders, and legs might join in the conversation. You are communicating that you are happy, angry, nervous, uninterested, or pressed for time. You telegraph your emotions to the listener. Depending on how good they are at reading it, they know a lot before and while you speak.

As a good *Listener* be aware of the body language of the receiver. It will let you read where the other person is coming from. You will know if "I'm fine" is true or is cloaking for an inner turmoil. By hearing the messages being sent you know how to respond.

Voice is another element for the Listener to remember. The speaker's words may be saying one thing, but their tone is sending a different message. How often were you told as a kid, "I don't like your tone?"

We instantly recognize the anger and resistance in a tone. The challenge for the good Listener is how to respond to it. It is natural for us to react in kind. If we do, we have escalated the issue, and listening has stopped.

One of the most valuable skills for an Involved School Librarian is knowing how to use the "pause." Think of the phrase "Stop! Look! Listen!"

As you pause, look at the multiple communications the speaker has been sending leading up to and including the angry tone. What were you being told?

In dealing with students, a soothing tone from you is likely the best way to calm the anger and defuse a possible confrontation. Coupled with positive body language, you will be able to discover what was the real trigger. You can then address a solution to the issue.

For something we do every day, communication can be a complex activity. To be a good *Communicator* and an Involved School Librarian, you need to be a skilled *Listener*.

Learner

Being a Learner is natural for all school librarians. We say we are lifelong learners. The competencies in AASL's National School

Library Standards[1] refers to learners not students. What about us as learners?

The world keeps changing and to keep up we must also be learners. It is why we librarians say we are lifelong learners. Our communities need to trust that we can help them with what they need or want to know.

The challenge is how and where we are to learn and what our focus should be. To be a *Change Agent* we need to know what needs to be changed. Often this involves knowing what is "next."

The business is always alert to what is "next," knowing their future depends on their ability to react to it. As a leaner we must stay on top of what might be coming next to identify its possible impact on the library, and what teachers and administrators will need to do about it.

To learn what might be next, subscribe to free online newsletters on technology and education. They will alert you to what is coming. The business section of the newspaper is another resource. When you find a potential future impact on the library and the school, explore it more deeply.

When you feel reasonably confident about the latest trend, schedule a meeting with your principal to discuss your findings. Here you need your confidence. If you sense resistance, don't argue, but don't retreat. Suggest you will investigate further to see if it's going to take hold.

As you learn more about the trend, update your administrator. Once it is likely to be the "next" thing, determine if it is just relevant to the library or if the teachers need to be readied for it. In the latter case, offer to give a workshop to prepare and support the faculty going forward.

In the process, you have shown your administrator that you are a valuable team member. This makes them more likely to support future requests from you. You strengthen the library, and your reputation as an Involved School Librarian increases.

Learners also have strong connections to their PLN. If you are fortunate, there are other librarians in your district. You have also made a connection with the public librarian. These form the base of your PLN.

The librarians in your state's school library association are the next level. Their resources and the librarians you meet at conferences are the next level. AASL and ASCD/ISTE build upon that. The national addition gives you further information about what is coming.

Not only will you know what is next, these connections also have webinars and presentations at the conferences giving you the training you need to develop proficiency with it. You are prepared to teach it to your colleagues and hold their hands as they integrate it into their practice.

Your PLN is there to answer any questions that arise as this new element is introduced. Remember it's good to have a plan to implement it, but you also need a plan to sustain it. That is until it is replaced by the next thing.

State and national school library associations usually have a presence on social media. Expand your PLN by joining their Facebook group. You might also join other state libraries' Facebook groups if they seem active.

Library-related blogs are another great addition to your PLN. AASL's *Knowledge Quest* has frequent posts. Find the most recent ones on their home page (www.aasl.org).

ISTE's home page features their latest blog posts. Scan down the page to Search Blog Posts. A search of Topics shows a list ranging alphabetically from Accessibility & UDL to Teaching Strategies.

ASCD (www.ascd.org) gives you a list of key words along with the number of posts on the topic. Since ASCD is the organization for supervisors and curriculum development, these give you a greater insight into what administrators are thinking about.

You will begin to see some regular bloggers. Contacting them is another way to expand your PLN. You might even write a post and expand your PLN that way.

Another source for your growing PLN are the special subject groups on Facebook. Consider joining the School Libraries Rock, Canva Librarians and Teachers (both moderated by Kristina A. Holzweiss), AI School Librarian, or my own School Librarian's Workshop. These gather and share information related to their focus. Mine is about leadership and advocacy, The hive mind is a great place to get answers to your questions.

The fairly new BlueSky is another social media site to explore. Much like the old Twitter, it is becoming more popular with those who no longer want to be a part of X. The Search feature allows you to select feeds, showing you the ones you like.

Look into micro-credentials. In addition to learning new skills, you get a badge or a certificate giving you documentation for your new knowledge. A few possibilities are the *Maker Educator Micro Credentials*(https://makered.org/professional-development/maker-educator-micro-credentials/), *Common Sense Educator* (www.commonsense.org/education/recognition-educators), and the *Library of Congress Professional Development* (www.loc.gov/programs/teachers/professional-development/).

ALA and AASL offer webinars and other online learning that give certificates. The *National Archives Professional Development* is similar to the one offered by the Library of Congress but they are given in several different locations.

One more thing to learn, and it's not likely to be something you considered: learn your library and the message it is sending. We go in and out of our library each day and don't stop to consider what it is saying to all who enter it.

Make it a practice once a month, perhaps the first Monday, to pause before unlocking the door. Enter as though you are seeing your library for the first time. What catches your eye? Does it support your Mission or take away from it?

Notice if there are distracting elements such as objects on a top shelf or furniture that partially blocks a smooth entrance. Is your display prominently positioned? How easy is it to see your Mission and Vision which you have hung on the library walls?

Consider your signage. Are you unconsciously using terminology that is a barrier to immediate understanding? Reference Desk is not as engaging as Help Desk. Instead of Circulation, choose Check Out.

The longer you work in a library, the less you see it. Your daily environment becomes so familiar, you don't see it through the eyes of students, teachers, and visitors. You want the library to reach out to them, inviting them to join you in their lifetime learning journey.

Remember change continues to occur. Sometimes fast and sometimes slow. The fast ones are easy to see. We know technology changes, but we forget different words and phrases have come into use and others have disappeared. We need to move with the changes.

We have become aware of how our inherent biases have affected our speech and perception of others. What we teach in history is a demonstration of these biases. What we are coming to realize is that the famed Dewey Decimal system is filled with bias.

For example, Dewey puts Religion in 200. Books about Christianity are classified from 200 to 289. "Other Religions" are assigned from 290 to 299. It is also American centric. North American History is assigned 970. Canada is 971, and Mexico is 972. U.S. History runs from 973–979.

Aware librarians, who listened to the silent message library was sending, began genrefying their collections. Books were given new headings and call numbers to reflect their subject. These were then arranged alphabetically. A huge task, but one *Listeners* know would send a message of inclusiveness to their communities.

The subject headings used by libraries have reflected these biases as well. The heading in the "Westward Expansion" does not reflect how Indigenous People see it.

Academic Librarians are seeing these biases in the Library of Congress System they use. They note how frequently "women" are listed compared with men. Men are seen as the predominant and women are a modifier. The same is true in the Sears List of Subject Headings used by public and school libraries.

Making changes here will be monumental. As a *Learner*, watch for solutions. You will be prepared for "what's next" in that basic library tool.

Once again, as Ranganathan said in 1931, "The Library Is a Growing Organism".[2] There is no stasis in life. If we are not growing, we are dying. And the Involved School Librarian is aware of the changes occurring and knows how and when to incorporate them.

Leader

We come to the third L – Leader. This is what the 5 Cs, 5 Ps, and the other two Ls have been preparing you to be. You undoubtedly are already a leader in many ways. However, by purposefully integrating the elements rooted in those letters you have become ready to be a *Leader* as an Involved School Librarian.

What does "involved" mean? According to the Merriam-Webster Dictionary,[3] one of its meanings is to be actively participating in something. It is what is meant in the title and how it is used throughout the book. It describes how you are as a *Leader*.

Think about the word "*Leader*." What comes to your mind? Do you picture a national leader, past or present? Perhaps a noted library leader is your first thought since you are reading about the multiple aspects of librarianship.

The word is defined by Vocabulary.com as "the one in the charge, the person who convinces other people to follow. A great *leader* inspires confidence in other people and moves them to action."[4] It gives some examples of use, such as being a "natural leader." Do you feel you are a leader or do you inwardly resist the title?

There are numerous reasons why you don't self-identify as a *Leader*. To get past that barrier, examine what constitute leadership characteristics. The Leadership qualities frequently mentioned are already embedded in what you have learned. One of the longest list I have found names these dozen traits.[5]

1. *Self-Awareness* – It comes from knowing who you are. Your strengths and weaknesses. In the first chapter on the 5 Cs, you discovered that and more, starting with *Confident*.
2. *Respect* – You show respect by being a good *Listener*.
3. *Compassion* – You express compassion through your ability as a *Listener*.
4. *Vision* – You created a Vision as part of identifying your passion.
5. *Communication* – As a *Communicator* you are now versed in the many ways you send messages.

6. *Learning Agility* – Being a *Change Agent* and *Learner* who keeps up with what's "next," you display learning agility.
7. *Collaboration* – Collaboration is one outcome of your being connected to your colleagues and *Purposeful* in working with them.
8. *Influence* – Again, being a *Change Agent* has you steering the direction of where things are.
9. *Integrity* – This comes from your values and includes your passion and your commitments.
10. *Courage* – Starting with Confidence and incorporating being a *Change Agent* demands courage, and you display it.
11. *Gratitude* – How you respond to others, saying thank you in meaningful ways, is an outgrowth of being a good Listener and *Connected* to the people in your life.
12. *Resilience* – Your resilience is embedded in your being *Confident* and your ability as a *Planner*. It requires adaptability to adjust to changing situations. Your ability as a *Change Agent* lets you recognize what is now needed and are prepared manage any setbacks.

This is an extensive list. Review it and see how the 5 Cs, the 5 Ps, and the first two Ls work together, making you an exemplary Leader.

Is that how you see yourself? We are *Confident*, but we don't always have enough confidence to think of ourselves as *Leaders*. Not being willing to take on that role takes away from our being *Powerful* and a *Change Agent*.

Your inner hesitancy is likely rooted in the stories you tell yourself. We love stories. They help us see the world in new and creative ways. But stories such as these are holding you back:

- *I don't have the time* – No one these days "has" time. We need to make time based on our priorities. Your Mission and Vision give you the motivation to do that.
- *I can't talk in front of groups* – You rarely need to talk to groups. When you do, you have something important to communicate. Your planning makes you ready to do so.

- *Leaders are born* – This is the big one. It's both true and not true. You can walk into a kindergarten class and identify the leaders. I certainly wasn't a *Leader* in my youth. Experience and learning combined to make me one. Time has tested you. Being *Passionate* and *Purposeful* have strengthened you. You are a *Leader*. You need to own it.

It's the stories that have continued to play in your mind that are holding you back. As you learned in being a *Communicator*, we are in constant communication. We forget that communication with ourselves is ongoing. In those communications we are inclined to negative self-talk that keeps us from leaving our comfort zone and trusting that we are the *Powerful* Involved Leader we need to be.

There is a tendency to retreat when one of your plans goes awry. Your negative self-talk gets louder. You acknowledged the possibility of the plan not going as proposed, but when it needs more than a tweak, you start doubting yourself.

Keep a digital or paper Success Journal. Record accomplishments, big and small, as they occur. Review the journal whenever you feel doubt creeping in. It will remind you that you have done it before. You can do it again.

Although we often tell students that Fail stands for "First Attempt In Learning," we rarely accept it as true for ourselves. Failure is scary. It makes us look bad. We do everything we can to avoid it. But it is also necessary. Without it we don't learn, and we don't get better.

Nothing great is ever achieved in one step. The steps along the way will always include some failures. And if you let the fear of failure get in the way, you will either back away from what you are doing when it happens or not start at all. As a leader, you need to take risks, and risks bear the possibility of failure. But without risk there is no reward – and no success.

Fear is part of the process – but it doesn't get to stop the process. Don't let fear of failure keep you from stepping out of your comfort zone. Accept the possibility of failing. Embrace that it isn't saying anything negative about you or your plan. Take a chance. Although you will fail sometimes, as you pile up your successes your reputation as a leader will grow – and so will you.

Think of leadership as an adventure, a journey with obstacles, achievement, and ongoing learning. We weren't told about this journey in library school. Indeed we weren't trained to be a *Leader*. We were taught pedagogy and librarianship – but not leadership. Many of us are uncomfortable about pushing ourselves to the forefront. Since childhood we have been trained not to be a show-off. It feels uncomfortable to praise yourself.

The good news is you don't have to be a braggart. Good leaders never do that. They let their work speak for themselves.

John Quincy Adams allegedly said, "If your actions inspire others to dream more, learn more, do more and become more, you are a *Leader*." That idea is likely embedded in your Mission Statement.

In accepting all that being a Leader implies, review what you know about power. Remind yourself what you learned in Chapter 2 about the powers you draw on:

- ♦ You have Power With. It enables you to communicate with others and build advocacy, knowing and sharing "together we are stronger."
- ♦ You recognize your Power To, which recognizes the potential of every person to shape their life and world. It's true of you as well as the people who join you in advocacy. This powerful inner force comes when you trust yourself. It makes you better able to utilize Power With – building the relationships and advocates for the library and its programs.
- ♦ Your strongest Power is your Power Within, the inner force rooted in your being *Confident, Committed, Passionate,* and *Purposeful*.

Take an inward look at how you are presenting yourself. Are you a *Leader* or a Manager? In practice, you need to be both but be aware of which roles you are doing. Determine whether it is the right one for the task at hand.

According to AASL's National School Library Standards, you are a teacher, instructional partner, information specialist, and program administrator. Each day you juggle those hats, but you are also wearing three more hats – Follower, Manager, and *Leader*.

You may not have spent much time thinking about these three hats, but they each can propel you forward as a *Leader*. In addition to recognizing that you wear these three hats at different times, it's important to be aware *when* you should choose to wear each one. Know **why** you are choosing it and how you will be acting either as a Follower, Manager, or *Leader*. How does your choice benefit the library program? How is your choice affected by living in a time of rapid change?

Being a follower has a negative image. Followers are sometimes considered to be non-thinkers and cowardly. If you follow, you don't have to make a decision. If you follow, you can't make a mistake. If you follow, it's less work. It's the easy way.

Yet there are times you do follow and need to do so. You know and accept that you are obliged to follow administrators' directives. But following is more than just doing what you are told.

I once heard a story that a college admissions director said to a parent, "Congratulations. In a class of 500 students, we have 499 leaders, but your child is the sole follower." And this was intended as a good thing. The admissions director recognized that following a leader is a learning experience. It teaches you the elements of good and bad leadership.

Ducklings follow their mother, learning what they need in order to safely reach duck adulthood. Elephants follow the matriarch, who is the oldest and largest in the herd. She is the one who can remember where the waterhole is that doesn't dry up in a drought. Her daughter follows.

In following your administrator, you can learn what, *other* than a title, makes people want to follow a given leader or not. You can identify good and bad leadership characteristics. You can discover what works when leading a meeting and what doesn't. A smart follower is always learning.

You are also a manager. You have no choice about managing, you must do it. This is about those many hats you wear in doing your job, and, in fact, you do manage every single day. However, there *is* a choice in how you go about it – on good days and bad ones.

On the good days, all the hats stay on you head in their proper positions. You manage effectively. Important tasks get done. You manage your relationships with teachers and students and create a positive environment. To the extent that you inform the administration of what you are doing, they see the library as working smoothly and being a contributor to the educational community. As a result, being a good manager promotes your program.

On the bad days, when you get buried under all the roles you have, your program pays for it. It's all too easy to become overwhelmed. In those times everything seems to be coming at you at once, and you can't keep track of what you need to do next.

When you reach that stage, your temper flares, you make mistakes, and you end the day feeling unappreciated, frustrated, and exhausted. If the administrator hears of it, you and your program have become one more problem for them to deal with. And you never want to be a problem for your administrator.

The truth is there will always be bad days. Everyone has them. And the occasional bad day won't harm your program. But if the bad ones are outnumbering the good ones, you need to adjust how you manage your workload.

Review your Mission. It grounds you. It lets you set priorities. Although there are times when you have to do things that don't connect to your Mission, it helps knowing that you are doing so. It puts what you are doing into perspective and should be an indicator of how much time and effort you need to put into that task. It also puts your daily tasks in context, letting you recognize how these tasks are helping you achieve your Mission.

A manager, whether at the corporate level or a librarian in a public school, is responsible for carrying out the Mission. You are responsible for carrying out yours.

Begin each day by quickly reviewing or saying your Mission Statement. If you haven't memorized your Mission yet, you soon will. Check your to-do list in whatever way you keep track of your tasks. Identify which ones best promote your Mission. Those are your focus for the day.

End the day the same way. Review your Mission statement. How did it go?

But what about the bad days? Do the same thing at the end of the day. You might be surprised at what did go well. And give yourself a break. No matter how good you are at managing there will be days that just won't work.

You create the Vision and the Mission. You do strategic planning and execute tactics to ensure the goal is achieved. In the business world You are the CEO and the COO of the library. In preparing and maintaining the budget you are the CFO. As a school librarian you are the entire C-Suite of the library.

For the library to be successful, you have taken on demanding roles. To be an Involved School Librarian you are always looking for ways to integrate the library into the work and consciousness of your different communities. It can be overwhelming.

Becoming overwhelmed will defeat you. Always include time for self-care. Whether you are refreshed by walking or doing yoga, put it on your to-do list to remind you.

Some of your self-care is daily, but longer weekly ones are also necessary. Perhaps you allocate time for pleasure reading on the weekends. Go out for lunch or dinner with family and friends.

Look for ways to bring joy into your life. Make it a priority. It will increase your resilience and add to your physical, mental, and emotional well-being.

Self-care makes you a better Leader. Being the best Leader you can possibly be is how you are able to be the Involved School Librarian. You and the library are viewed as essential and valued by your communities.

The 3 Ls are very personal. They are how you are inside as you present yourself to the outside world. *Listener*, *Learner*, and *Leader* are all present as you draw on the 5 Cs and the 5 Ps. Get ready to bring them to your communities.

References

1. AASL (2018) *National School Library Standards For Learners, School Librarians, and School Libraries*; ALA Editions: Chicago, Ill.

2. Ranganathan, S. R. (1931) *Shiyali Ramamrita. The Five Laws of Library Science*; Edward Goldston, Ltd.: London.
3. Merriam-Webster (n.d.) *Involved*. Retrieved March 27, 2025, from www.merriam-webster.com/dictionary/involved.
4. Vocabulary.com (n.d.) *Leader*. Retrieved June 16, 2025, from www.vocabulary.com/dictionary/leader.
5. Center for Creative Leadership (2024, July 3) *12 Essential Qualities of Effective Leadership*. Retrieved March 25, 2025, from www.ccl.org/articles/leading-effectively-articles/characteristics-good-leader/.

4

Reflect on Yourself

You have taken a deep dive into who you are. You discovered the necessary attributes you already have and those you should strengthen or develop to be the Involved School Librarian. Reflect on all you have learned.

The three previous chapters explored much that you already knew. The structure placed these elements in a new context. First by looking at them in isolation to hold them up for a closer look. Next they showed how the letters in that chapter built on each other sequentially and then explained how they related to each other in a different order.

This organization pattern illustrated the important characteristics of each letter as well as its impact in combination with the others. With each succeeding chapter, the connection between letters from previous chapters was indicated.

The whole is greater than the parts. The chapters demonstrated what it takes to be a school librarian fully involved in the communities they serve.

Consider how it will impact on your thinking and your behavior as you interact with your communities. Where are you now? What needs to change?

Think, Create, Share, Grow, the four domains of AASL's National School Library Standards[1], serve as an excellent guide. Reflect on the domains and competencies for learners as that is where you are at this point in your journey as an Involved School Librarian.

Think – Learners display curiosity and initiative.

- What are you now curious about?
- What word or words from the 5 Cs, 5 Ps, and 3 Ls sparked a deeper interest?
- What questions do you have and where will you go to find answers?
- How does what you have learned fit in with previous knowledge?

Create – Engage with new knowledge by following a process.

- What are you planning to do next?
- Which of the three letters will be most involved with what you are planning?
- What format will you choose to create this plan?

Share – Adapt, communicate, and exchange learning produces with others in a cycle.

- With whom and how will you share your learning?
- Who will be the best audience/receiver of your plan? Students? Teachers? Administrators? Parents? Other community members?
- What feedback would you give to the author of this book?
- How do you now expect to react to feedback from others? What, if anything, is different from the past?

Grow – Participate in an ongoing inquiry-based process.

- Where and how will you continue to seek more knowledge? Your PLN? Your state and national library organizations?
- How will you incorporate this continued learning into your professional life?
- How will you demonstrate your new understanding in your work world?
- How will you use reflection to help guide your future decisions?

In Parts II and III you will put Part I to work by exploring how to draw on the attributes and strengths you have discovered and become a fully Involved School Librarian.

Reference

1. AASL (2018) *National School Library Standards For Learners, School Librarians, and School Libraries*; ALA Editions: Chicago, Ill.

Part II
Involving Students, Teachers, Administrators

You know your strong and weaker attributes. How will you bring the strong ones into your work life? Each day, you deal with students and teachers.

You come into frequent contact with your principal and vice-principal, if you have one. On more rare occasions you will see your superintendent and assistant superintendent, the latter again if you have one in your district.

Each of these interactions are opportunities to build or expand numerous means of becoming more valuably intertwined in what they are doing. You help them achieve their goals and feel successful. In the process you become the fully Involved School Librarian.

The route to this interconnection with the school community is through implementing the 5 Cs, the 5 Ps, and the 3 Ls.

5

The 5 Cs in Action

You have seen the 5 Cs in yourself. Now see how you can implement them in your interactions with the school community. These are the people with whom you are in contact on a regular basis.

From *Confident* to *Change Agent* we look at how each of the Cs can impact students, teachers, and administrators as you become the fully Involved School Librarian.

Confident

Students
The students are your highest priority. Your work with teachers and interactions with administrators are all part of how you ensure that students are prepared to learn and grow intellectually and ethically and are prepared for an undefined future. You guide their journey, *Confident* in knowing you create the opportunities needed for them to discover and navigate the world of information and ideas.

The first and biggest challenge you face, no matter what the level of your library, is that the students coming into the library are not yours. At the elementary level with a fixed schedule, at best you will see students for about 45 minutes once a week. In some districts you may see them once every two weeks or less. Getting to know each student is not easy. Nor is it a simple matter to fit in time for book return, a lesson, book selection, and checkout. And then the next class arrives.

In middle and high school, unless you have a special course to teach, which does happen, you have even less frequent contact. You see students when the teacher brings the class in. The purpose may be for the class to do a research project with you only giving the initial introductory information or for several days with you and the teacher working together.

Sometimes the teacher doesn't want you to do anything. (And you have to work to change that situation.) There is no one set way. It will be different from one teacher to another. And it very much depends on how proactive you are.

Middle and high school students also come in individually. Most often it's during lunch, but it may be to complete something at the direction of a teacher. While these students are in the library, you may be involved in teaching a class. In addition to possibly helping this drop-in, you must also not allow that to be a disruption to the class you are teaching.

If you are not sure of yourself, Confident in what you know and how you can help them achieve their goal, they are not going to trust you. It is important never to be over-confident. True Confidence recognizes that it doesn't know everything.

Recognizing that limit is a positive. By your behavior, you show them that the object is to learn, and you are a learner just as they are. Having the same challenge forms a connection, aiding in creating the feeling that the library is a safe, welcoming space for all.

What do you do when 25 or more students come into your library all at once? Whether they are dropped off by the elementary teacher or accompanied by the middle and high school teacher, they are in your space. You are responsible.

If you are not Confident, your instinctive reaction is to try to control the situation, and that's a mistake. You need to manage, not control. Trying to control will bring the opposite of what you are trying to achieve and won't make the library feel like a welcoming space.

Rather than controlling, you want to manage the library environment. Remember what was discussed in Chapter 2 about the three types of power. *Power Over* is about control. It suppresses initiative, produces resentment, and, often, rebellion. None of which you want in your library.

Power Within is trust in yourself. It is rooted in self-confidence. It is what allows you to manage situations.

Power With is even stronger and is an outgrowth of Power Within. When you are *Confident*, you can easily connect with others and draw out their best. When you work with students to foster their Power Within you encourage their initiative and curiosity, engaging them in learning that's meaningful to them.

Using Power Within and Power With is also the way to prevent or minimize students regarding time in the library as a free period. After all, you are not their teacher.

Being *Confident* is the first step in managing your multi-faceted interactions with students.

Teachers

Most of your access to students is through the teachers. Their perceptions of you range from a valuable, knowledgeable colleague to someone who runs the library. They may or may not trust your ability to teach their students. At the elementary level, you are often seen as the "special" who gives them their break.

How you react to the attitudes teachers have to librarians will determine what comes next. It's easy to feel if a teacher doesn't want you to help, so be it. You have plenty of other jobs to do. But that emotional response keeps you from making the teacher's students your primary task.

In the most extreme dismissal of your abilities, observe the class. Take note of the purpose of the library visit and its connection to the curriculum, what the teacher expects of the students, and what sources are used in the lesson. When the class is over, comment on how well-behaved students were.

Look for the resources you would have used had you been part of the lesson. Send a brief email to the teacher suggesting it as a follow-up or when it will be taught again. Keep the tone as a suggestion, not as pressure to be included next time or imply that the teacher didn't do a good job.

Get to know the teachers personally. What are their interests outside of school? Send a note if you find something that relates to this. Slowly build a friendly presence with them.

Listen to conversations to find out what is being taught next. Send an email with some possible resources to use. Offer to teach that if there is interest.

Relationships are built slowly. They are personal as well as collegial. You will always be closer with some teachers more than with others, but the library serves everyone.

Administrators

Being *Confident* with your administrators is not always easy, particularly if you are a new school librarian or new to the school. You don't see them daily, unless your principal makes a practice of welcoming everyone as they sign in. It's easy being *Confident* in those friendly morning greetings.

It can be a challenge to be *Confident* when your principal enters the library. Administrators come into the library for one of two reasons. They are either showing a guest around the school or are going to assess a lesson you are teaching.

When the principal brings a guest and you are in the middle of a lesson, simply acknowledge their presence with a nod of your head and a smile. Continue what you are doing until you reach a point where you can step away from students. Then welcome them and ask if they have a question or need anything.

In the interchange, you radiate your *Confidence*. They have come into your space, and you know what you are doing and why you do it. If the opportunity arises, point to your Mission and Vision Statement posted on the walls.

The principal's visit for an assessment is usually scheduled. You are asked if the preferred time works, particularly if you are in the middle or high school as you aren't always teaching. Since you know about it in advance, you can easily prepare for it.

Do a handout stating the goal of the lesson, what has proceeded it, and what will follow. If you collaborated or cooperated with the teacher, include that information as well. This is an opportunity to showcase what you bring to students and teachers.

At the end of the class, ask the principal if they have any questions. Praise any connection you have had with the teacher in preparing the lesson. By doing so, you strengthen your relationship with the teacher and show you are a team player.

On extremely rare occasions, your superintendent may come into the library. They are usually accompanied by the principal and may also be bringing a guest. While this can feel more intimidating, you have already established how to react based on previous visits by your principal.

The superintendent usually, but not always, remains until the end of the class. If they do stay, use the same follow-up you did with the principal's visit.

Draw on your *Confidence*. You know what you are doing and why. Remember to record these administrator visits in your Success Journal.

Committed

Your commitment is formalized in your Mission Statement. It is your "Why" for doing what you do each day. You live it every day.

Students

Your students see your Mission Statement hanging on the wall every time they come into the library. Few probably see it as more than the furniture and other components of the library, but the words are there in their subconscious mind. What happens when they are in the library is what brings it home.

A project on misinformation and disinformation gives them the tools and knowledge to navigate this complex information world that has built-in traps to snare them. When they do an inquiry-based assignment on a topic connected to their classwork, they learn to locate information and use it ethically in the process.

Listening to stories at the elementary level and discussing what they learn from it, looking at how the illustrations convey meaning, and sharing their ideas sparks a lifetime love of reading. Displays on topic, whether they are of fiction, nonfiction, or a combination of both, extend their interests and give them a broader perspective on literature.

When students see books that portray other cultures or ones which feel comfortably like their own, the library collection gives them windows and mirrors. They see the library as a welcome and safe space for all. In the process, they get a better understanding of their community and develop empathy for others.

Recognize what your contributions are to student learning. When you have a particularly good project or class, record it in your Success Journal. Reflect on what made it so successful.

Teachers

They may not have a written Mission, but good teachers are committed to their students' success. When you collaborate with them, first acknowledge a part of the proposed learning experience that connects with your Mission. This gives you the opportunity to suggest additions and/or modifications to what the teacher has conceived.

In your discussions use phrases such as, "I know you want …" or "I recognize your commitment to. …" Follow it with how you feel the same way. Refer to your Mission Statement and go from there.

Identifying your common purpose in working with students forms the basis for building a relationship. The trust inherent in relationships results in more occasions when you work together. All of which brings your Mission to a continuing reality.

Administrators

As part of their responsibilities, your principal will observe you several times in the course of the school year. At the elementary level, the secretary usually will alert you to the upcoming visit. At middle and high school levels, the secretary will call to ask when you are next teaching.

Principals evaluate you based on what they know from their own teaching experience. They are not aware of the range of responsibilities included in being a librarian. You will have to expand their appreciation for what you do.

When they come to observe you, provide them, probably as required, with your lesson plan. They are not likely to see it as your Mission Statement in action. It is in the discussion when they give you their assessment that you have the opportunity to explain it.

If you have figured out you principal's "Why" for their job, point out how you both work to make your Mission a reality. Invite them to come back for a broader look at how you carry out your Mission. At that time you can show any displays or special areas such as a Makerspace, explaining their part within your Mission.

In sharing your Mission with administrators, you build their awareness of what you do and why it is of such importance to students and teachers. As a result, you become important to their success.

Connected

To be a fully Involved School Librarian, you need to build connections to everyone in your building. While you would do much of this naturally, it's important to be focused on doing so to ensure that you are reaching the maximum number of individuals.

Students

In addition to being your highest priority, students are the biggest challenge to becoming Connected. There are far more students than teachers or administrators. How do you make connections to so many of them?

As always, start small and continue working on it. Greet students with a smile when they come in as a class. Make brief positive comments on something they are wearing. Offer something about yourself in return.

Note the natural leaders and those who are loners or noticeably unpopular. Observe their behaviors, what books they like, what interests they seem to have. When the opportunity arises, suggest a book they might like.

A non-reader who loves sports may like a biography of a favorite player or a website on a sport they love. Ask them for recommendations as well. Knowing that you are interested builds a connection and makes them open to what you have to offer them in a lesson. The connection lessens the possibility of them disrupting the class for any reason.

Consider forming a library council if one doesn't exist. Talk first to the principal about the best way to go about it. Middle and high school students usually have a free period during which they can volunteer in the library. High schoolers like the opportunity to put this on college applications.

Students from fourth grade up can be helpful. The challenge is to find a time when they can come. I had such a council for years. An extra benefit is that the students tell their parents about it, spreading the word about the value of the library.

Teachers

Teachers come in small packages. At the elementary level there are grade level packages. At middle and high school levels there are subject area packages. You need to connect to them in their group package and as individuals.

To connect with them based on their group, consider what part of the collection deals with or is appropriate for what they are teaching. Suggest picture books for a kindergarten or first grade teacher to use. Depending on whether you use Dewey or are genrefied, share titles recently added to the collection or an update to a database their students will need.

If it can be fitted into the schedule, offer a workshop for teachers to discover the additions. Give them time to look through the offerings. Otherwise let them know that you can give them one-on-one time or insert it while their students are working on a learning project in the library.

Involve them when you are discarding books. Explain the bases you use when considering a book for discard. Some will want your discards, perhaps to re-use in an art project or because they love the book for some reason. Just properly stamp it and let them have it.

Use any shop teachers you might have to help you make decisions on what to discard. A woodworking teacher was horrified to discover that some of my oldies had illustrations of people working without masks or goggles.

Make a connection with the specials. You might create a project with the art, music, or physical education teacher. I have worked with all three in a joint school-wide project.

Don't overlook the Nurse and Guidance Counselors. They bring their own knowledge base. You can make sure you have material for them in the collection, and they might be able to help you with student needs.

Remember, you are not doing all this at once. It is a step-by-step process. Over time you will have made connections with the entire faculty.

Administrators

Making connections with the principal is vital. How they view the library and the librarian is based on their previous experiences. You want to make sure that they recognize and count on what you bring to students' growth.

If you belong to ASCD or ISTE-AECT you are keeping up with the topics of importance to them. You also become current with their latest buzz words. This forms a basis for connections.

From their communications to the staff and comments they make at faculty meetings, you can identify their goals. By knowing their wants and needs you can address them in several ways.

You may come across articles or blogs from the business or tech world that relate to those goals. An email with an attachment will demonstrate you are aware of their challenges and are prepared to help. You may not get a response but keep doing it. Not so often as to be a nuisance. Just enough to show your support.

If you know their personal interests and/or hobbies, pass along information you find about those as well. These connections create a collegial relationship which leads to the principal developing a positive view of you and the library. They also help make the principal look good in their own relationship with the superintendent.

Communicator

Your ability as *Communicator* is where the rubber meets the road. Chapter 1 discussed Gary Harzell's prophetic article on the "Invisible School Librarian." The Involved School Librarian is anything but invisible.

Remember the tree falling in the forest. Your skill as a *Communicator* ensures that the whole school community hears the noise. They become advocates for the library and you.

Promoting the library program does not require you to brag about it. It needs you to demonstrate how it serves students, teachers, and administrators. Communication is not always about words. It is also about actions.

Students

Showing your value to the school community always begins with your students. For these learners to discover why the library is important to them, you need to know who they are.

Build your background knowledge. What are the demographics of your community? What attitudes are they potentially bringing about the library?

Observe their clothing. Do their t-shirts carry messages you can use to open a conversation. Perhaps they are wearing a team logo. Are they fans of a rock group? Tap that information to suggest a book they might enjoy.

When students come to the library as a class, once you and/or the teacher have gotten them started move around the room to see how they are doing. Look for ways to briefly and positively interact with them.

Ask guiding questions to help them get past any obstacle they have encountered. Specifically praise good thinking. Also comment on how they are managing the assignment. Note if they are using past knowledge to handle it. Praise how a group is working collaboratively.

Depending on how often teachers use the library for their classes, you might begin to see the same students working in different subject areas. Ask which subject is their favorite. All this helps you get to know them. And it helps them get to know you as a person as well.

You have opportunities for more interactions when students come in individually. Find out if they are looking for something specific. They may know just what they need and go to the right place but check in to see if they could use more information.

If they seem to like one author or a genre, suggest similar authors. Always avoid becoming a nuisance. Respect their privacy.

Over time, students will build their trust in you. They may not state it this way, but the trust leads to them perceiving you as necessary for their personal growth.

Teachers

Although we speak of them as a group, teachers are individuals. Their attitudes towards their job, their students, and you are rooted in previous experiences and their emotional responses to them. To communicate with teachers, you have to get to know them.

Start with teachers who have the most positive feelings about the library. It is easier to feel *Confident* when you are dealing with people who like using the library professionally and personally.

What can you do to increase their connection to the library? When they approach you about bringing in their class for a project, look for ways to take the assignment deeper. Use the Shared Foundations and Key Commitments for Learner in AASL's National School Library Standards[1] to guide your thinking.

Share your ideas and the Standards with the teacher. Be sure to include a student-produced visual demonstrating their learning. This, along with what the teacher will share with their colleagues, will help promote the library with those less library-inclined.

Hopefully, your next outreach will be with those teachers who liked what they heard about the project you have just done. Share the students' culminating visual. Listen carefully to what the teacher has in mind.

Avoid criticizing any part, simply add your recommendations. If they are rejected, don't object. Present the library component as the teacher wanted. At the conclusion, suggest that the next time we might be able to broaden the learning, The use of "we" is key. You want to foster and grow your cooperation.

Wait until you have built successes with teachers before taking on the most resistant to the library. When signing in or out and at lunch, listen to learn what they are working on now or planning next.

Send brief emails or put a note in their mailbox with a small suggestion. Invite them to the library to find out more. And have coffee and snacks available when they come.

They may ignore your first and second attempts. Don't be a nuisance but be persistent. Eventually, your reputation with other teachers and your efforts will pay off.

At the elementary level, send teachers ideas for follow-up activities to a library lesson or a story that you told their class. Invite teachers to see your latest acquisitions. Again, have coffee and food available. Let them borrow whatever catches their attention.

Step-by-step you can involve your library into the practices of all the teachers.

Administrators

You have been connecting to your principal by keeping them posted about potential forthcoming changes. As a *Connector*, you demonstrate being a team player, helpful in keeping them ahead of the game with the faculty and the superintendent.

In your role as a *Communicator*, you keep the principal informed about the library. All too often, you are overlooked as your principal focuses on the teachers and what is going on in the classrooms. It's up to you to keep them informed about what is happening in the library.

What, how, and how much you communicate requires balance and an awareness of the principal's needs and preferences. Subject, brevity, and frequency are key.

Focus on student learning and teacher creativity and success. You are showcasing the value and vitality of the library without saying so.

To keep it brief, use visuals such as infographics and formatting to send the most important messages. While a template for your infographic may seem like a good idea, the sameness over time can cause the principal to overlook parts of it. A few pictures of culminating student products are good, but don't include all of them.

Remember the principal is very busy and so are you. Aim for monthly reports. If that is too taxing, do it quarterly. But do it.

The principal will come in to observe you several times a year. Most of the time these are scheduled, although you might be told by the secretary that it will occur at some time during that day. If you are asked to provide a good day for the observation, you will only be able to suggest something within the next few days.

Take charge of how you are evaluated by inviting the principal to view a specific lesson. Be sure to inform the teacher about the upcoming visit. When they come in, give the principal a one-page summary of what led to the lesson including teacher cooperation/collaboration, the targeted learning outcome, and formative/summative assessments.

In addition to demonstrating your expertise, you have once again made a teacher look good. The principal is likely to praise the teacher for their contribution to the lesson. They will also hear from the principal because of your regular reports. The result is that teachers see multiple benefits in working with you.

Another positive outcome is that the principal might include information about the lesson or something from one of your reports in their own communication with the superintendent. This helps to build your reputation as a significant contributor to student success.

You have gone beyond ensuring that the tree makes a noise if it falls. You have built advocates who will work to make certain that the tree won't be cut down.

Change Agent

To be a *Change Agent*, the 5th C requires you to utilize the other 5 Cs as you continue to move your library forward. Most people don't like change. It upsets their world. The tried and true feels safe, change is uncertain.

For an Involved School Librarian, change is a natural and ongoing part of how you operate. Chapter 1 cited Ranganathan's fifth law of library science, "The Library Is a Growing Organism." The first chapter also discussed Gary Hartzell's article "The Invisible School Librarian." If we are to survive and thrive, we must change.

We are lifelong learners and recognize that our world changes daily. The business, tech, science, and political world are constantly transforming our lives. It takes a while before most people become aware of something new happening.

Librarians need to be ahead of the game, ensuring that our library is positioned to be an active participant. We must be ready to incorporate the "new" into our program and lead our school community to benefit from the change.

Change involves risk, and most people are risk averse. You need to be *Confident* to change the failure. The truth is, not every change works. You have to keep your commitments in mind as you connect with students, teachers, and administrators. And you must communicate clearly with them.

Students

Your commitment to making the library a safe, welcoming place for all students is a crucial area for change. It is an ongoing process as there are numerous ways to improve on what you currently do to create that environment.

Does your collection represent the student body? Even if it did, populations change over time. Demographic shifts may mean you need to look for resources to meet the new needs.

Are you fully addressing accessibility issues for students with disabilities? Physical issues include wheelchair use, keyboard requirements, and ease of reaching shelves.

What do you need to learn about neurodiverse students? While physical disabilities are easy to see, neurodivergence includes autism, ADHD, dyslexia, dysgraphia, dyscalculia, Down Syndrome, and others that are not obvious. Speak with the guidance counselor to learn who these students are and what accommodations you need to make.

Pay attention to how others are treating them. You can't just insert yourself to protect the student without making the student feel like more of an outsider. The guidance counselor and the teacher can help with creating strategies to deal with the issue.

Making the library a safe, welcoming space means addressing DEI. Each of those three letters gets more specific. **D**iversity is about representing the many differences in the school population. **E**quity means ensuring that all students get what they need in a way that addresses their area of diversity. **I**nclusion means that everyone is made part of the whole.

But for your library to be truly welcome to all, add a "B" to DEI. "B" is for **B**elonging. Belonging means everyone feels safe to speak their mind.

Use your connection with students to guide you in planning your next step. Soliciting student input will keep you in touch with what else needs to be included or discarded from the library program. A library council is one way to have them keep you alert to the next changes to make.

When the members of the library council feel trusted and know you value their suggestions, they will alert you to areas you may have completely overlooked. Additionally, they are early adopters of new tech and are happy to show you what is great about them and how to use it. Then you get to bring it to the rest of the school.

Do surveys every so often. Seeing that a suggestion is implemented will encourage more participation in the next survey. On occasion, you might focus on an area of the library you think might need updating. Should the signs be clearer? Are the activities such as makerspaces still popular? Should something be added?

If you haven't genrefied, try asking if students would like to have the library switch from the Dewey Classification. (Make sure your administrators are aware of your plans and the reasons for it.) Should you make that move, you might be able to enlist student help in tackling the gigantic process. If you are genrefied, is there a genre that should be added or changed?

When you make a student-suggested change to the library, post a thank you to them on your website and on a library sign.

It will keep the discussion going and add to your being involved in their lives and their involvement with the library.

Teachers

Teachers tend to be resistant to change. Why add more work by adding something new that alters routines and introduces new practices? Things were running fine.

Attempting to introduce a change against that mindset will not get you supporters. Instead of attempting to reach all the teachers at once, target the early adapters. There are always a few teachers who love to try new things.

These teachers will listen and embrace new ways to make learning more interesting, relevant, and to fine tune the change. With each tweak, you learn how to approach introducing the change to the remainder of the faculty. The teachers working with you will help by talking with other teachers at lunch, on duty-free periods, and other times when they are casually together.

Slowly the word will spread. Your next approach might be teachers who are not adamantly opposed to change. Possibly, they may come to you after having spoken with one of the early adapters.

How this works depends on the scope and nature of the change. Some changes, like using AI to create lesson plans or formative and summative assessments, can easily be introduced one-on-one. Other plans, such as genrefying the collection, affect everyone at once.

Dealing with the latter case requires planning how to get buy in by everyone as well as how to accomplish the project. You will need support from the administrators, but that doesn't mean the change won't result in anger from resisters. And it won't do much for maintaining and building relationships.

Again with support from the principal, address the reason for the proposed change at a faculty meeting. In advance of the meeting, actively solicit input from all teachers as to why they don't like the idea as well as what they like about it. The hard core won't like anything about it, but that is to be expected.

Chart the pros and cons as expressed by the faculty so it can be seen visually as well as hearing what you have to say. After introducing the teachers' views, add the reasons you chose to make the change.

For example, if you are genrefying to address the bias in the Dewey Classification system, the most notable areas are Religion (200–289 for Christian Religion) and History of North America (973–979 for U.S. History). The imbalance lends credence for the change. Sharing the list of genre headings used shows how much more accessible these are than Dewey to student needs and interests.

Administrators

You cannot change anything significant without involving the administrators. Getting their support for a change doesn't begin with scheduling a meeting with them to present your idea. It starts long before.

Building the relationship that creates the foundation for having your principal and possibly your superintendent supporting the change you are proposing takes time. You don't see administrators as often as you see teachers. How long I will take to develop the relationship is dependent, in great part, on their previous experience with librarians.

What you have been doing as a *Confident, Committed, Connected Communicator* is what has paved the way to get their approval for your proposed change. By now you know their needs and wants enabling you to show how the change will forward them. Scheduling the meeting is the next step.

You never want to have that all important meeting take place on a Friday afternoon. Everyone, including the principal, is looking forward to the weekend. I once had a meeting to see my superintendent on a Friday afternoon. Her secretary cautioned me not to take up too much of her time. The superintendent replied, "I told you, if Hilda was coming to see me on a Friday afternoon, it is only to give me good news."

This is also a reminder to use the secretary's knowledge of the administrator's schedule. Ask them what a good time for the meeting would be. You also need to be mindful of your own schedule.

When you have a huge change in mind, the best meeting time is during the summer. They are working, but their schedule is not as hectic as it is during the school year. While you will be succinct and focused as you present your idea, the discussion isn't rushed. There is time to talk about budget implications and adjustments that can be made.

In the fall, your budget preparation will go smoothly as all the potential concerns have been addressed. Your focus can now be on creating a timeline for the change and preparing the faculty for what will be happening.

Being a *Change Agent* is not easy but the library must change for it to grow and continue to be relevant to users. As you can see, to be a *Change Agent* you must be *Confident, Committed, Connected,* and a *Communicator*.

The result will involve a 6th C – Culture. You are creating a library culture with the shared values of intellectual curiosity and a love of literature and learning. Everyone belongs and feel welcome and safe.

Reference

1. AASL (2018) *National School Library Standards For Learners, School Librarians, and School Libraries*; ALA Editions: Chicago, Ill.

6

The 5 Ps in Action

We now look at the 5 Ps: *Passionate, Purposeful, Planner, Professional,* and *Powerful* and how they further your involvement within the school community. The Ps complement the Cs as they blend emotions with goals. In combination, you gain the extra strength needed to power you forward.

Passionate

Students

In the words of Theodore Roosevelt, "People don't care how much you know until they know how much you care." Connections come from emotions. Assignments are too often disassociated from students' interests. They do or don't do them based on how important the grade is to them.

Because you care about what you do as a school librarian, you also care about your students. They are your reason for being. How do you reach out to them to show how much you care?

Unlike classroom teachers who may have 25 to 150 students, depending on whether you are in an elementary, middle, or high school, you have the entire school population. Getting to know them and letting them get to know you is a top priority. It won't happen overnight but making it part of what you do every day will get you there.

Start with a smile. When students come in as a class, be at the door to welcome them with a real smile. Find something brief to say to as many of them as possible.

Comments about a t-shirt, outfit, or a new haircut are the easiest. You might say, "You are looking happy today. I hope to add to it." If you see a downcast expression or body language indicating sadness or worry, you can say, "It looks like your day isn't going well. Maybe we'll be able make it go a bit better."

Once the class settles down into the lesson, move about, observing and letting them know you are there to support them in doing their best work. As you are doing so, watch the interplay between students. Who are the leaders? Are any being left out?

Let the leaders know that their input is helping others. Speak to anyone being ignored by the others and engage them in a brief conversation about what they are doing. Offer suggestions about the project rather than referring to their separation from the class. They are aware of that. Your focus is on showing your interest in them as a student and person.

The challenge for you as a school librarian is being simultaneously aware of any drop-in students. This is particularly true in middle and high school. Have they signed in? Do they seem to know what they are doing or do they need help?

The library is a large open space to supervise. Students can be quite inventive in finding places to hide out. If you notice one or two attempting to be invisible, find out why they are in the library. Keep your tone friendly, asking if they need any help.

Look for opportunities to give students a voice in the library. Ask for volunteers to create a display or bulletin board tied to one of their interests. This is a chance for them to share their passion and creativity. Invite the principal to see it.

Try a bulletin board asking, "What's Your Favorite …?" and then adding several possibilities such as genre, author, song, or musical group. Have a place for them to submit their responses. At the end of the month, or whenever you are getting the next bulletin board ready, post a summary of responses and include your own.

As a follow-up you might do book displays based on their favorites. When students see their interests included in the library it adds to their feeling the library is a safe and welcoming space. The library becomes intertwined in their lives.

Teachers

Teachers often feel underappreciated. They are overburdened and tired of shifting priorities from administrators. Since the pandemic, the behavior and motivation of their students has become a serious issue. Student absenteeism is at an all-time high.

That description is similar to what you as a school librarian face. While it may seem tempting to use your commonalities to commiserate with them, it won't bring about positive results. Instead, reach out to teachers through your passions.

Teachers have their own "Why" for choosing their profession. Like yours, it's rooted in the desire to make a positive difference in students' lives. Use this shared "Why" to work with them to create learning experiences that ignite student interest.

As discussed in Chapter 5, you build relationships with teachers one at a time. In proposing a project or new technology to integrate into an upcoming unit, speak to their "Why." Recognize how hard they work and how overworked they are. Make it clear from the very beginning that you will be doing the heavy lifting.

Assure them you will deal with any aspect of your suggestion that they feel is extra work or out of their comfort zone. You are the extra pair of hands they need. If you have done this or something similar with another teacher, mention that as a reassurance.

Share what was the inspiration for your idea. Was it something another librarian did? Did you read an article about it? You want them to feel secure that the project won't go south and create more problems.

When the project is completed, inform the administrator, highlighting the teacher's participation and the resulting student learning. The principal will most likely find a way to complement the teacher for the project. Knowing you were responsible for the principal's reaction makes the teacher more willing to work with you on your next idea.

Every successful project builds trust, and trust is the foundation of relationships. Word spreads among the faculty, paving the way for more projects with more teachers. Teachers eventually come to you with ideas of their own. You have become fully involved in their work life.

Administrators

The high turnover in administrators is an indication of their own feelings of being overworked and unrecognized for their contributions. The superintendent wants evidence from the principal to show district goals are being met. Parents call or come in only to complain, never to praise. They are suffering from burnout.

The revolving door of principals is an opportunity for you to make an early connection from which you can build. Most new principals begin their job in the summer, which as previously noted is the perfect time to meet them. While they are busy settling into their new position, they still have more time than when school begins.

Be mindful of their time but use what is available to acquaint them with the library program. Whatever their previous experience with librarians and library programs, you want them to know what drives you and how it plays out daily. Let them know that you will invite them to see you in action.

While the purpose of the meeting ostensibly is to inform the principal about the library, it also provides the opportunity for you to learn about the principal. You should be able to glean some idea of their needs and wants.

Like teachers, principals have a "Why." Most often it's a positive one, although there are some whose "Why" is negative. The positive ones are seeking to lead the school population in creating a culture of learning and literacy. They want students to feel their teachers care about them, and the teachers to be forward looking in preparing students for whatever the future brings.

A few principals like the power the title brings. They are authoritarian in their approach, although they often put on a mask of caring. Inevitably, they create a toxic environment. Teachers start looking to retirement. And you should consider looking for another school library position.

Both types of principals like the positive messages you send them. Those who want to create a culture of learning and literacy appreciate knowing the school is on the right track. The power loving principal likes the information you send because it improves their position with the superintendent.

Emotions are a powerful force. Knowing where yours are based and recognizing the ones that motivate others will guide you on your journey to become a fully Involved School Librarian.

Purposeful

Chapter 2 introduced the link between being Purposeful and being Committed. Your passion for what you do combines with your purpose, enabling you to bring your commitments alive and your Mission meaningful in your interactions with students, teachers, and administrators.

Students

From the moment they enter the library, you want them to know they are welcome and safe. The library is a haven and a wonderland. It's where they are free to discover themselves even while working on a learning experience.

It's easy to create that feeling at the elementary level when you are reading a story that will take them into deeper thinking. The challenge is to make their visit a wonderland or an opportunity for self-discovery when they are there with their teacher for a project.

Generally, the teacher has begun the assignment in class and placed students in groups if they are expected to collaborate. Your opportunity comes when you introduce the library portion.

Ask some questions designed to get them thinking about what they will be doing next. For example, if they are working on an English project related to authors of a particular time period, you could ask, "What challenges do you imagine the author might have had that are similar to something you might face? Where do you think you can find out?"

It isn't necessary for them to answer, just think about it. Ask only a few questions and then launch into how and where they can find what they need for the project. You want them to begin with an inquisitive mindset but not take time away from them getting started.

The purpose to your introduction is to guide students into making their work personally meaningful. Assignments should not be about completing them, although that must be accomplished. They should be an integral part of students' own journey into lifelong learning, developing a curiosity about their world and how it came to be.

Bring your purpose to students who come to the library individually. Their time may be limited or can last for the entire period, depending on who sent them and why they are there. Learn what that is as soon as possible so you can help as necessary.

While helping them find a book to borrow, discover their interests and be ready to suggest what they might like next. If they have come to research something specific, find out why they are looking for the information. As with the class, ask a few questions to get them more personally connected to what they are learning.

This is the library wonderland. Everyone's journey is unique. And all journeys are welcome.

Teachers

Most teachers are as passionate about what they do as you are. It may be hard to recognize when it's buried under their feelings of being undervalued and overworked. You reach them by bringing their hidden passion to the forefront.

When they are discussing an upcoming unit at lunch or have come to see you to schedule their class, ask what they are hoping students will get from the unit and/or project. Acknowledge them for what they are trying to accomplish. Then add the ways you can help with it.

At first it may sound like more work to them. Just what they don't need. Once again, reassure them that you will be the one doing most, if not all, of the additional work. Suggest that while in the library, they can catch up with paperwork since you will be managing the students settling into project.

Talk about the culminating assignment. Even if there is a paper involved, suggest a visual element as well. Add that you would love to display them in the library.

Showcasing the students makes the teacher look good to colleagues, a department chair if there is one, and, of course, the administrator who you will invite to see it. You will have reignited the teacher's passion. You are also expressing your passion.

When teachers get in touch with their passion, they experience a sense of joy. Coming to work each day gives them pleasure. Their feelings are communicated in their teaching.

A joyless teacher results in joyless students. The opposite is also true. In bringing joy to their day, their library visits become a wonderland and an opportunity for their personal journeys and growth.

This is the ideal. It won't happen every day. But the more you bring being *Passionate* and *Purposeful* into your relationships with teachers and students the more often it will occur.

Administrators

To connect with administrators, you must first identify their needs and wants. Some of course are only seeking power and a bigger paycheck. Most truly want to make a difference, creating a learning culture where students are growing intellectually and reaching for their dreams and teachers bring their best to students each day.

This is more of a Vision than a Mission. It can never be fully realized. There is always more that can be done. But it is what the best administrators are seeking.

Competing with this purpose is a more practical one. Budgets are a constant presence in their lives. Everyone wants something. Budgets in general are getting tighter. Even in places with strong financial support for schools, there is never enough to cover all the requests.

They face difficult choices on a daily basis, and too often must disappoint teachers or even students. The principal has to respond to pressures from the superintendent. The superintendent has to deal with the Board of Education.

Political forces are making a tough job even tougher. It's no wonder that the turnover in administrators is so high.

How do you as an Involved School Librarian see this as a "chopportunity?" From finding grants to tech products and alternatives that address the money crunch, your skills as a librarian can speak to those key needs of administrators. The success of incorporating your finds creates a connection that gets you increasingly heard.

When presenting your idea to your administrator, show you recognize and understand their purpose and passion. Say something like, "I know how much you want to. …" Your suggestion then is seen as less of a request and more of a solution. With so many problems, administrators need all the solutions they can get.

You won't be doing this often, but it will add up. Beginning by appreciating the difficulties of the administrators' jobs you adjust your mindset in how you interact with them. As you continue to do so, you adjust their mindset as to how they see you and the library fitting into their goals.

Planner

Planning is embedded in all you do. With the complexity of managing all your roles, it is a necessity. The better you become at planning, the more successful you are.

Two notable quotes embody the importance of planning. "If you fail to plan, you are planning to fail." And in the words of the famous Yogi Berra, "If you don't know where you are going, you will wind up someplace else."

Students

You do have lesson plans for what you are teaching students. You probably have a library curriculum. If you don't there are plenty available online for free or fee. But your planning needs to be broader to increase your impact and increase student engagement.

How old is the curriculum you are using? Who wrote it? Analyze it to see if it's addressing all that it should, furthering students' self-discovery and interests as well as reaching learning goals. Does it address information digital literacy? From third grade up, students should be ready to use AI and do so ethically.

For all your teaching, use AASL's National School Library Standards[1] as a guide. You should have a copy of it, but the downloadable framework at the Standards landing page (standards. aasl.org) is sometimes easier to use.

Try to get copies of the curriculum for all grades or subjects. This alerts you to what students are studying and when. With that in hand, you can adjust your lessons to reinforce and complement their classroom work.

Teachers

Speak to or email teachers when your lesson with students connects to what they are teaching. Knowing what you have done helps them in further developing the unit they are working on. It also opens the door for you to plan lessons together.

At the elementary level, planning is limited to cooperative lessons. The class time with you is the teacher's free period. They need that time to get caught up with their work or just de-stress.

Connect with the other "Specials." They share your challenges of dealing with the whole school population. A portion of their students are highly interested in the subject but others are disinterested.

Collaborate to plan a unit involving art, music, library, and even physical education. When you plan together you see the many ways you can support each other. The resulting projects unite the school, bring out talents and creativity in students, and show the value of "Specials" beyond giving teachers a duty-free period.

Both cooperative and collaborative plans are possible at the middle and high school level. In the first case, the teacher introduces the project in class and may even have a starter activity. Then the students come to the library and you do your part.

A collaborative unit may or may not start in the class but you and the teacher determine what and how each of you presents the lesson. Together you identify the desired learning outcome, what curricular standard it meets, and how it will be assessed. When at its best, you both circulate among students as they work on the project.

Whether you work cooperatively or collaboratively, planning together is an opportunity to get to know the teacher better. Although planning is not considered an emotional activity, when you are working with someone else, emotions always are present. Being aware of that correlation increases the quality of the project and sets the stage for future planning together.

Shape the lesson or unit to align as much as possible with their passion and purpose. It shows you know and respect what they do. Tweak it as you go along to ensure that the desired outcome is achieved. Any credit for the success of the project goes to the teacher.

You don't need to praise your work. It will be obvious and noted. The more successes you have with joint planning, the more other teachers will be open and willing to work with you. Little by little you have become fully involved in how teachers work.

Administrators

Planning is a fundamental part of an administrator's job. Your planning for the library must connect with what they do. The first rule for you is to always keep them informed. Good or bad, you have to let them know what is happening in the library and to what purpose.

Getting their approval for your plans depends on how they fit into the supervisor's wants and needs. Your track record is another consideration. You have built a connection through your monthly or quarterly reports. They are aware of your reputation among the faculty. All will help further any requests and/or ideas you present.

Recognize that the principal has to answer to the superintendent. For a big project that may involve a high cost, knowing the superintendent's wants and needs helps you frame your proposal. Timing is also critical. If it doesn't fit into the budget cycle, your plans will have to be postponed for a year.

From interacting with students to making a huge change such as genrefying or physically expanding the library, you need to be a *Planner*. Your plans come from your passion and purpose. You craft your plans by yourself, but small or large, you draw on the relationships you have built with students, teachers, and administrators.

Professional

Think of words to describe yourself? Did you list *"Professional?"* It should be included in your self-view as it affects how you present yourself to students, teachers, and administrators. When that is part of your mindset, you communicate your passion for being a school librarian and are *Confident* in the value of what you bring to the entire school community.

Unlike some professions, your dress doesn't announce what you do. School librarians can dress very casually, have tattoos, and other fashion statements that aren't usually associated with being Professional. It doesn't take away from how they are perceived as long as they imbue professionalism in their interactions with others.

Students

You are there as your students' trusted adult friend. You have made the library a safe haven. The students feel close enough to tell you private information so that you can help them. But your *Professional* presence ensures that the relationship never crosses the line into a personal friendship.

The ALA ethical standards are foundational to your teaching so students learn how to use, create, and share information. These standards are seen in action as you build a library collection that mirrors the student population and the world around them. It does take being *Confident* and *Committed*, requiring you to know yourself and what you won't compromise.

In "providing equitable service policies," school librarians work to eliminate barriers to library use by students. Fines are eliminated and methods are in place to manage the financial burden of replacing lost books. They keep current with information on how to best serve students who are neurodivergent and those with physical challenges.

Teachers

You have been demonstrating your professionalism in your interactions with teachers. You have earned their respect for what you bring in the way you work with them to plan learning experiences. In taking the responsibility to teach and manage the portions of the project you suggested shows them you keep your word.

Too often school librarians are seen as an extra. Not much different from a paraprofessional. Your goal is for them to see you as their *Professional* equal. You create that trust in how you have helped them achieve the desired outcomes of lessons. They then come to recognize what you do as a skilled *Professional* to make their work easier.

Years ago, I left one library position for another. I sent notes to the teachers with whom I worked most frequently and heard many express sadness that I was going. One sent me a letter in which he said, "You are the ultimate pro. You gave me the opportunity to work at my level and at my pace."

By seeing teachers' passion and giving them opportunities to display their professionalism, you are a gift. It's worth all the time and energy you put into it.

Administrators

Administrators recognize and admire Professionals. It is a mark of quality. They want the competence and skill implicit in the term to permeate the teaching and develop students to prepare for their future – and who do well on standardized tests that get publicity. You have been demonstrating your own professionalism in keeping them informed through regular reports and the projects you have done with teachers.

Being active in your library association is another way to show you are a true *Professional*. Write an article for their journal or do a blog post. Then make sure they are aware of what you have accomplished. When you participate on a committee or take on an office, you or the association will usually inform your administrators.

If a new administrator is hired over the summer, schedule an appointment as noted earlier. Keep it brief. They are snowed under as they take on the responsibilities of their new position. Let them know you will invite them to see a library class later in the school year.

Follow up on that invitation in a few months. If you are inviting the superintendent, let the principal know. Have a brief handout for the administrator giving any background information on the lesson, the intended learning outcomes, and any other relevant information. Send a message, preferably handwritten, thanking the administrator for coming.

Two letters I received from one superintendent demonstrate the value of creating this connection. After seeing a class, she wrote,

> It is always a delightful experience for me to see the operation of a learning experience, particularly when it's a good one. I was delighted to see that particular class work with enthusiasm amongst the books and through that, hopefully, retain some of my conviction that books will remain important for at least the rest of my lifetime experience.

In the letter the superintendent wrote after she learned of my first publication, she said, "I would be remiss if I did not congratulate you on your achievements. The school district is fortunate to have someone with your *Professional* stature on the staff." Having administrators know and appreciate what you do smooths the way for all your planning and makes it easier to get budget requests approved.

Powerful

The word "power" conveys strength. Believing you are powerless keeps people from achieving all they can do and be. Chapter 2 reviewed the different types of power and which ones will promote school libraries. As an Involved School Librarian, you need to access your own power to show students and teachers they can reach their goals and create greater ones.

Students

Far too many of your students feel powerless. It is the root cause of numerous disturbances along with frustration as they attempt to use "Power Over" which is so often used on them. The solution is to give them "Power Over."

In this instance, Power Over is giving them voice and choice in their library learning experiences. First there can be a choice of topics within the framework of the project. Also allow the culminating work to be done in a variety of forms which can be open to student choice.

You may have envisioned a standard paper to complete the project, but a video, podcast, well-designed work of art, or other possibilities can achieve the same purpose. Additionally, going beyond the traditional approach allows neurodivergent students to tap into their own talents and skills. Offering alternatives and being open to student suggestions on what they might do gives them "Power To."

Give students a rubric tied to the desired outcomes. Once students are underway, speak with them as they work on their chosen project. Keep them focused on what they need to show or demonstrate to meet the goals.

As students become involved in their creation, you have also given them "Power Within." They develop confidence in their abilities and see themselves as successful and capable of dealing with obstacles. These are valuable life lessons that go well beyond the information they learned in completing their project.

Teachers

Tightly structured curriculums, changing administrators, and pressures from parents create a sense of powerlessness in teachers. They don't become disruptive, but they are frustrated and stressed. The joy and passion that led them into teaching is just about gone.

Use your relationships to connect teachers back to their passion and restore their former sense of power in their work. Review their curriculum to see when a new unit will be starting. Let the teacher know that you are there to help them reach their desired outcomes.

Go one step further. Engage the teacher in a conversation about what they love and don't like about the unit or its structure. What did they enjoy about teaching the unit in the past?

Once you have identified the "what" that formerly made the unit a positive experience, look for opportunities where the library can build in alternatives to restore that feeling. Tie into your PLN to learn if any librarian has had a successful experience working cooperatively or collaboratively on that unit with a teacher.

Bring what you have discovered to the teacher and begin planning what you can do together. As with students you want to incorporate multiple options. By increasing student engagement, you add to teachers' enthusiasm – and joy.

When teachers feel stressed they tend to resort to "Power Over." This often leads to disruptions causing them to use more "Power Over." Teachers are unhappy and so are students. Learning doesn't flourish.

Just as with the students, in designing a unit with more options built-in, the teacher now has "Power To" and "Power Within." By using your "Power Within," you have become more valuable and involved in how the teacher approaches new units and lessons.

Administrators

Administrators are well aware of their power. What is important is for them to recognize and appreciate your power. You are a potential ally for them. On the other hand, you don't want to ever be seen as "teacher's pet."

Use the power you have built in your relations with administrators to be an ally for teachers. You are in a unique position to interpret an administrator's planned initiative to make it palatable to teachers.

A superintendent I once had, not the one previously mentioned, believed "if something isn't broke – break it." He was espousing the idea that "good is the enemy of great." His word choice was not the best way to get teacher support. Before he proposed anything, the teachers were opposed to it.

He wanted to alter how teachers taught and evaluated students. Several surveys were conducted to allegedly get teacher input on the new approach. Needless to say all responses were highly negative. However, from the way and by whom it was introduced, I knew his plan was a done deal.

As both a teacher and administrator ally, I scheduled a meeting with the superintendent. Rather than endorse his plan, I suggested I acquire resources to help the teachers make what would be required changes. Knowing my past history, the superintendent approved my idea.

I also got funds to purchase whatever materials I would need to support the teachers. In addition to getting the resources, which included information I obtained from my PLN on how the approach was implemented in their school, I offered workshops and one-on-one tutorials.

The teachers were relieved they would have help and wouldn't be left to cope with making the change. The administrators were relieved they wouldn't have to deal with a rebellious staff. I ended up with an enlarged budget which I could use as a baseline for future budgets as well as having the teachers and administrators know I could make their lives easier.

The real-life experience illustrates the strength of "Power With" and "Power To." Using those two forms of power drew from "Power Within" – being *Confident*. We are very Powerful when we know how to use it.

From *Confident* to *Change Agent* and *Passionate* to *Powerful*, you can see how these qualities make you an Involved School Librarian. Now see how 3 Ls take you even further.

Reference

1. AASL (2018) *National School Library Standards For Learners, School Librarians, and School Libraries*; ALA Editions: Chicago, Ill.

7

The 3 Ls in Action

Three more attributes will complete what you require to make you a fully Involved School Librarian. As a *Listener* you gather the understanding to support students, teachers, and administrators achieve their goals. As a *Learner* you acknowledge you don't know everything, but the more you learn the better you can identify the resources your community needs. As a *Leader* you create a forward-looking inclusive culture that recognizes your value and that of the school library.

Listener

Students

From the moment they walk into the library, students are communicating with you and you are doing the same. Bring your active listening skills, particularly the non-vocal ones, to identify those who seem to be angry or struggling. In the first case, you are prepared to deal with a potential disruption. In the second case, you know you will need to provide support and extra guidance.

Notice how students are interacting with each other. Is one being ignored? It's easier for some students to engage in bullying when in the library. It's bigger than the classroom. You aren't their "real" teacher. Time for some fun.

Again, by observing interactions, can you identify a positive leader? Your ability as a *Connector* will let you use that student to get the class focused and on track.

Be aware of your body language. A welcoming smile, that you mean, comes first. Your *Confident* mindset sets the positive tone needed for all. It will also ensure that your tone sends the message that you are looking forward to working with the class.

Listening to what students are saying provides you with a formative assessment of where they are in their learning and how they are progressing throughout the lesson. Knowing where students are allows you to adjust the planned project. You can then provide scaffolding or challenges to guide students into achieving more than they thought they could.

As always, keep your ears open and be aware of student drop-ins. Do they appear to be working purposefully? If a singleton student seems to need help or be refocused on getting work done, you are ready to move to them once the class is working on their assignment.

Teachers

Listen carefully to what teachers say when they come in with their class or alone as well as their offhand comments in the cafeteria and when signing in and out. Stress is widespread so you will hear a lot of grumbles and gripes. When a response from you is required, acknowledge you hear their frustration but don't add your own issues. Your answer might be repeated, and you don't want others to hear negativity from you.

Do be aware of their body language and respond to indications of their anxiety and tension. Offer whatever help you can to make their lives a little easier.

I once saw a teacher walking through the hall with her body radiating exhaustion and sorrow. I invited her to come to the library and have coffee in my office. I also always had snacks available for teachers.

When she came in, she felt safe enough to reveal what was troubling her. It was a medical issue about a family member. Just unburdening herself was something of a relief. Now someone else knew. I also let her know about library resources that might give her more information.

Administrators

Pay careful attention to whatever administrators are saying verbally or in their written communication. Listen to what is being said and not said. Pay attention to their body language and whatever it is telling you.

By listening intently you can see whether things are going well or whether there is a change in the winds. Is the administrator pleased with what is happening? You can potentially identify possible departures or budget cuts.

Your skills as a *Listener* allow you to position yourself as best as possible to whatever is about to happen. You can prepare how to turn it into that "chopportunity" to promote the library or safeguard your funds. Pivoting is more successful when you are able to anticipate what is going to happen.

Many, many years ago, I was in a district where the administrator had decided to move the school onto block scheduling. That meant classes met for a double period. In this version, a student's schedule for the year was divided in half. In the fall semester they would complete all the work for half their courses. In the spring they would complete the remaining courses.

Because I knew the administrator's wants and needs – his goals – I knew the decision had already been made. Just as with the situation in Chapter 6 on changing teaching and evaluation methods, they weren't looking for teacher participation in the process.

The teachers in different departments continued to argue, explaining to the administration why this was a bad idea. I was a sympathetic ear to the teachers but avoided agreeing with them as it would have been reported as joining their protest. I knew the change was coming.

I spoke to my administrator, pointing out that fear and uncertainty was part of the resistance. Teachers logically worried how to teach one subject for 80 minutes to high school students. They were sure the kids didn't have an attention span that long. As in the other situation, I suggested if I had supplemental funds,

I could purchase resources on teaching in a block schedule, and even have the material include subject specific information, shelving them in a special area for teachers. I got the funds. The teachers got the resources. Both the administration and the teachers saw me as being supportive. That is using your skills as a *Listener*, *Communicator*, and *Change Agent*.

Listening is at the heart of your leadership skills. It's also at the center of building the relationships you need to be successful as a *Leader* in a school. Take the time to listen to others and yourself and you will make a greater impact.

Learner

Students

The AASL *National Standards for School Librarians*[1] generally uses the term "Learner" for students, but we are all learners. As librarians we can learn so much from our students. We strive to prepare them for their future, and in a way they are already there.

The line from "Getting to Know You" in Rogers and Hammerstein's *The King and I* correctly says, "If you become a teacher, by your pupils you'll be taught" (Rodgers & Hammerstein, 1951). We tend to joke about how knowledgeable they are with technology, but you can learn much from them.

My students were the ones who showed me AlltheWeb. It was the second internet search engine and the first to work very smoothly. It began in 1999 and lasted until 2011 when Yahoo bought it and closed it out. When subsequent developments occurred, my students kept me informed and as a result, the teachers and administrators saw me as an expert.

Working with my students on their research papers, I learned as much as they did. From a student doing a math research paper, I learned that Arabic numerals came from India. While subject teachers are aware of new developments in their field, I was learning about them in all areas.

Being open to having your students teach you shows them we all must keep learning. It also shows them you value them and recognize their abilities. The connection this forms creates a positive environment for teaching and learning lessons.

Have students teach what they have learned or created as part of an inquiry-based project. Experiences such as that show them the value of learning. They are on their way to becoming lifelong learners who will probably be learning from their future children.

Teachers

You learn from students and you learn from teachers. They are the masters in their subject or grade level. Ask questions to learn more about the topic and what the teacher wants to accomplish.

Find out if this project has been done before. If so, what were the results? Was there anything that disappointed the teacher or was particularly successful? If it's new, what do they hope to see in the students' products?

What concerns do they have? From there you can find out if there are any essential questions for it. If not, make some suggestions and ideas for how the project might be altered and what parts you will take on.

Find tech resources that will showcase what students do and be shareable on your website and any places where parents and others can see it. Be sure to offer to check students' works cited information.

Your responses to the information they shared with you lets you explain the resources that will work best with the learning experience for students and/or lets them know how you plan to use them in teaching the class.

Use your skills as a *Listener* while discussing a new project. Listening actively and deeply will make the collaboration work more smoothly. Honoring the teacher's knowledge makes them willing to plan more units in the future.

The teacher also knows the students in their class far better than you. They have developed techniques that work with any neurodiverse students they may have and ways to deal with those likely to be disruptive. This knowledge will help you do a better job with the class.

At the conclusion of the project, ask what the teacher would have liked you to do differently. You are opening yourself to some negative feedback, so be prepared. You need to learn what works with this teacher.

Don't defend but offer some alternatives to what you can do. By being vulnerable, you have made it safe for the teacher to explain their wants and needs in a project. You can now freely offer your ideas as they can accept, reject, or modify them in a conversation built on trust that leads to more collaborations and stronger relationships.

After a first project with a teacher, send them a handwritten thank you note. Congratulate them on what their students achieved. Send an email to the administrator complimenting the teacher. It is ongoing and sometimes slow, but you are building a culture of collaboration.

Administrators

Your reports and messages inform the administrators what you do and need to do as a school librarian. Depending on the relationship you have built, you might share materials from the AASL National Standards Landing Page (https://standards.aasl.org).

More importantly you learn from your administrators. As part of your advocacy efforts you have used your ability as a *Listener* to discern your administrator's goals. But learning goes two ways here as with the rest of your community.

Your administrator is a model – good and bad – for what makes a *Leader*. I had one principal who had a strong ego. He expected everyone to do exactly as he said because he was the boss. He actually referred to himself that way on occasion.

The result was that teachers did what they were told. But they didn't do more. He had squeezed the life out of their creativity. The teachers suffered and so did their students. By contrast, I had a principal who would send "Kudos" acknowledging achievements of teachers and their students. Teachers felt their work was respected and strove to do more.

A superintendent gave me the best lessons in leadership. In a district that voted down school budgets regularly, she had mastered the art of effective compliments. They were specific and made teachers feel proud. She would use a past compliment as an opening to a request for Teachers to volunteer to do something that another district would pay them to do.

Her tight budget also had her turn down most requests for projects that required funding. However, if you came back with an alternative she was more likely to agree to it. I asked her about that, and she told me when people come back having tweaked their original idea, she knew they were serious and committed to its success.

The lesson I learned from her is, if you don't ask, the answer is always "no." And once you ask, there may be a way to turn a "no" into a "yes."

Leader

Students

During your interactions with students, either individually or as part of a class, you can tell who the natural leaders are. Connect with them as part of your presentation to engage them in the activity. Most of the remaining class members will naturally follow.

Identifying the *Leaders* is easy, even more important is showing the other students their own leadership abilities. It is your job as a *Leader* not to create followers, but more *Leaders*. This idea is in line with my life mission, "I reflect back to others the greatness I see in them, and when appropriate help them manifest in their life."

Students observe teachers all the time and make judgments about them. You have learned about the different forms of power. Which one you choose will affect how they see you.

As a *Leader*, you never want to resort to "Power Over" when dealing with students. Coming from "Power Over" is not how you want to be seen or as you want to see yourself. You don't want students to learn that is what Leadership is.

Instead give them opportunities to have choice and voice the library learning experiences. This gives them "Power To."

Every time students experience a positive power and finds it rewarding, they, as the rest of us, look for ways to make it happen more often.

You are a role model of a *Leader* for students, as are the teachers. They are not consciously aware of doing so, but they are learning from those who have control over their life. You want to be an example of a good, motivating *Leader*.

In the words of Dolly Parton, "If your actions create a legacy that inspires others to dream more, learn more, do more and become more, then, you are an excellent Leader." True for your students and true for you.

Teachers

In leading teachers, you start by knowing them. You know their leadership style. You are aware of what types of power they use. And you know their "Why" and what constitutes success for them.

You have been listening to what they say and then do. You have been learning about them from all your interactions with them from the casual to meaningful conversations. Through this you have built a relationship with them, stronger with some than with others.

Start with the ones with whom you have built the strongest connections. At the high school level, listen when they come to schedule a class project. You want to know what they want the learning outcome to be.

Your response should be, "You are covering important ideas and concepts. I can expand on them by …." You never want to dismiss or minimize their plan. You want them to perceive your contribution as support to make the project better.

It's not always easy to hold back your initial rejection of what they have in mind because it didn't require students to think and generate new ideas. Too often teacher projects have the equivalent of "only one right answer." However, you will not get them to revise it by dismissing their approach.

While you can present a library curriculum at the elementary level without collaborating with teachers, being involved with what they are teaching in their classroom will further student learning. It will also result in teachers who value your input and expertise.

The definition I highlighted in Chapter 3 (from Vocabulary.com) is, "A great *leader* inspires confidence in other people and moves them to action." By being a *Listener* and *Learner* in your interactions with teachers you become a valued, Involved School Librarian.

Administrators

The administrators are the official *Leaders*. They certainly have Power Over through their title. Through your reports and occasional scheduled meetings, they now perceive you as an invaluable resource for advancing their needs and wants.

You have used your attributes to learn what these are. Put them all into action. You will need the information to lead them to approve your ideas and plans addressing your needs and wants.

Whether you need and/or want the library to have student or parent volunteers, host an author visit, genrefy the collection, or even plan a renovation, any change may be outside the administrator's comfort zone. (They have theirs just as we do.) Prepare well. Be sure to tie your presentation to their needs and wants.

Have an overview of your plan as well as details in case they want to see it. You need to convince the administrator that you can bring it off. Bring your Confidence.

Watch their body language as you make your pitch. Listen to any reservations and objections they have. It they reject it outright, rework it based on what they said. Then return with your revised pitch. Your resilience and commitment stand a good chance of gaining their approval.

We started with confidence which every leader needs. But it takes more than being *Confident* to be an Involved School Librarian. Now you have added being a *Committed*, *Connected Communicator* who is a *Change Agent* as well as being *Passionate*, *Purposeful*, and a *Planner*, a recognized *Professional* and *Powerful*, along with being a *Listener* and *Learner*, enabling you to be the *Leader* integrated and involved with the whole school community.

Reference

1. AASL (2018) *National School Library Standards For Learners, School Librarians, and School Libraries*; ALA Editions: Chicago, Ill.

8

Reflect on Your Involvement with the School Community

Time for a pause. Look back on Chapters 5 through 7. Review how the 5 Cs, 5 Ps, and 3 Ls have reframed how you need to be as you ensure you are Involved in your school community.

Think, Create, Share, Grow – the four domains of AASL's National School Library Standards[1] – serve as an excellent guide. Reflect on the domains and competencies for school librarians and school libraries as that is where you are at this point in your journey as an Involved School Librarian.

For your reflection, use the four domains to identify where you need to go next. Here are some questions and ideas to get you started.

Think

- How can you give students more voice and choice in their work and in their sense of ownership of the library?
- Which teachers do you need to target to encourage them to collaborate with you? How are you helping them incorporate new information and technology into their teaching?
- What can you do to improve your communication and connection with your administrators?
- What else do you now feel needs more attention from you?

Create

- Develop a plan, including your Mission and Vision to have *student* library assistants.
- Conduct a survey on what students would like to see added to the library or a book display they would like to create.
- Launch a monthly alert to teachers about helpful websites and tech news. Offer to give one-to-one help to whomever would want it.
- Design a template of an infographic to give your administrator a monthly report highlighting student achievement, teacher successes, and collaborative projects.
- What else do you need to create to promote the library?

Share

- Have students contribute to a bulletin board about the best book they read recently.
- Invite teachers to share their students' latest projects in the library and invite your administrator in to see it.
- Send links to your administrator about new developments in the tech and business world that might soon impact education.
- What else might you share to keep your school community informed and prepared?

Grow

- Explore how to best meet the needs of neurodiverse students to ensure they feel safe and welcome in the library.
- Build new connections and relationships with special education, art, music, and physical education teachers to learn how the library can better serve them and their students.
- Read minutes of school board meetings to see where emphasis is being placed.
- Subscribe to online websites or print journals directed at administrators.

- ♦ Work on time management strategies to be able to add these plans into your life. Be sure to include time for self-care.

Expand your involvement by using the 5 Cs, 5 Ps, and 3 Ls to develop the library's presence in the larger community and create supporters for it and you.

Reference

1. AASL (2018) *National School Library Standards For Learners, School Librarians, and School Libraries*; ALA Editions: Chicago, Ill.

Part III
Involving the Larger Community

As an Involved School Librarian, you can't be insular. Your school community is where you work, but larger forces are involved in your life. Reaching out to the outside community and becoming a known and important part of it will strengthen the library. In doing so, your Mission is seen as vital, and your Vision comes closer to reality.

Picture a bull's eye. In the center is the library program. There are three rings around the bull's eye.

The innermost ring is you as you have seen in Part I. You have addressed the attributes associated with the 5 Cs, 5 Ps, and 3 Ls that you use in your interactions with all your communities.

The second ring was the school community. You discovered how the 5 Cs, 5 Ps, and 3 Ls were needed as you worked with students, teachers, and interacted with administrators.

The third and final ring is the community outside the school. First group is the parents. They entrust their children to you. Censorship has always been a part of what you must handle with them, and it now has become even more critical these days. But parents are the greatest advocates for the library. See how the 5 Cs, 5 Ps, and 3 Ls can help you make that an actuality.

The second group is the larger library community. They fully understand what you do and the challenges you face. Your connection to this community brings you support and ideas to lead, manage, and improve your library. Here, too, the 5 Cs, 5 Ps, and 3 Ls help you get the maximum possible results.

The third group is the business community. It is a reach to form connections with them, but they are voters. Your relations with them can affect their support for the budget and you. Use the 5 Cs, 5 Ps, and 3 Ls to make them library supporters.

9
The 5 Cs in Action

Once again we return to the 5 Cs to see how using the attributes from *Confident* to *Change Agent* can position the library in the larger community – the one where the school is located and the Professional Community to which you belong. It ranges from almost next door to the world itself as you explore the many ways you can become involved. Some bring you advocates. Others are sources of learning helping you grow.

Confident

As soon as you go outside the school community, you are leaving your comfort zone. You will be speaking and interacting with parents, the library community, and the business community. When you feel insecure, remind yourself of what you recognized about your inner confidence in Chapter 1.

Parents
In your contacts with parents, you will find some who are *Confident* – they believe they know better than you what is best for their child's learning and growth. While it's great to feel *Confident*, this is one area where confidence is regularly misplaced.

Parents in the first group are the ones most apt to keep their child from reading some books. When it is a simple case, you can assure the parent that you will not permit their child to borrow books the parent finds offensive or inimical to their child. This will take care of the usual challenges.

The problem arises when they want the book removed from the library. It has become more prevalent as the political climate has stirred up fears. Be prepared for how you will react and deal with the parent.

This is always a stressful situation for a school librarian and even more so today. It is where you need to be *Confident* to navigate the discussion. Your calm demeanor will keep the discussion from getting overly heated.

You should be prepared for how you will respond. The first step is having a selection policy you can share with the parent. You may also want to say that other parents might want their child to have access to books on that topic and others this parent finds objectionable.

While this may diffuse a few challenges, the parent who is charging you with promoting sexuality will probably not give up the battle. In denying the charges the parent is making, avoid repeating the words they used. You don't want those words coming out of your mouth.

Reply calmly, explaining that the school library is for everyone. Keep going. Use the phrase "a safe, welcoming environment." Add that it is a place for learning and inquiry. Your even tone of voice will make it harder for the parent to continue the diatribe.

These parents will leave unsatisfied, often with a threat to take the matter further, potentially to the next Board of Education meeting. This is a frightening scenario for school librarians but preparation helps.

Whether the challenge was handled easily or ended with the potential for it to be on the agenda of the next Board of Education meeting, you need to inform your administrator as soon as possible. You should never blindside them. Being the bearer of bad news is difficult but giving them a heads up is better than having them be caught unaware.

You don't have to face this scary situation alone. There are ways to get support. Your first supporters are the majority of parents.

This first line of defense is one you have been forming using the 5 Cs, 5 Ps, and 3 Ls. This, and subsequent chapters in Part II, will have you prepared. These are the people who will show up at the Board meeting and speak positively about you and the library.

Library Community
Welcome! This is home. You are a member of this community. It is your safe place and your learning place.

You are *Confident* with the others in this community. Being a part of it also offers you opportunities to build your confidence. We are stronger together and help each other to be even stronger.

There are three parts to this community. The first is the public library. It is the one your students and parents use along with the rest of the municipality you are in. Whether there is only one or there is a branch that serves your school population, you need to visit and meet with the librarians there and get your own library card.

Depending on the level at which you work, invite the children's or the youth/teen services librarian to your library. You both should know where each other "lives." Are there services the public library has that would be of interest/benefit to teachers?

Find out how many of the teachers are members of the public library. Prepare a joint flyer inviting teachers to sign up for library cards. Would the public library display student projects if teachers are interested?

The next part of the library community is your State School Library Association. If you aren't a member as yet, you need to join.

Your State Library Association has an assortment of resources for members. They invariably have conferences and webinars designed to extend your knowledge, boosting your confidence as you better serve your school community. Make attending the conference a priority.

Some State Library Associations provide information on dealing with book challenges and how to report them. Typically they also have various grants and awards you can apply for.

See their Vision and Mission statement, list of committees, and members of their Board of Directors so you are familiar with what they stand for and the people leading the association.

The third part of the library community is at the national level. You should be a member of the American Association of School Librarians (AASL) as it is the only national organization focused exclusively on school librarians. *Knowledge Quest* (*KQ*) is its bi-monthly journal. The articles connected to the different themes of the issue keep you on the cutting edge of school librarianship, building your confidence in what you do and where you want to go next. The *Knowledge Quest* blog appears a few times a week with bloggers describing their experiences, giving you practical advice on what you can add to your program.

When you join, you also join the American Library Association (ALA).

Be *Confident* in the face of book challenges with ALA resources on banned books (www.ala.org/bbooks). Look through the Book Résumés link on the page for ones that have been challenged in your library. The résumés give you the "significance and educational value" of the title. Use it in a discussion with your administrator and possibly supportive parents before an upcoming board meeting. The information will give you the confidence you need if you attend the meeting and speak up.

ISTE is the International Society for Technology in Education (https://iste.org/) and is where the technology part of the school library connects to a larger community. The site lists their blog posts, podcasts, courses, books, journals, and more. Browse by topic or job using a list of topics to explore.

Both AASL and ISTE publish national standards. The 2nd edition of AASL's National School Library Standards was published in fall, 2025. It is not a re-write but rather what is called a "refinement." As the advance notification stated, it has "updated context, clarified language, and enhanced tools to help you apply the frameworks with greater confidence and purpose." The Standards landing page (https://standards.aasl.org) provides resources and guidance on implementing them.

The ISTE standards include those for students, educators, and education leaders. The website states the Standards "provide competencies for learning, teaching, and leading with technology, and as a comprehensive road map for the effective use of technology in schools worldwide." Resources for implementing the standards are on the Standards home page (https://iste.org/standards).

ASCD (Association for Supervisors and Curriculum Developers) is your connection to what Administrators are focusing on. It publishes numerous books dealing with issues relating to different grade levels and administrator leadership. See Resources (www.ascd.org/resources) for a list of their latest. Joining will get you their monthly journal *EL* (Educational Learning) which will give you the vocabulary to use when communicating with administrators.

IFLA is the International Federation of Library Associations and Institutions (www.ifla.org/). It is your window and possibly your entry to librarianship at the global level. Explore the website. The range it covers is huge. Make it more manageable by exploring the School Libraries section.

Business Community

While this won't be a high priority area for you, don't overlook it. If you live in the community where you work, it is easy to be familiar with businesses. You use many yourself.

For those who don't live where they work, build in some time to become acquainted with local businesses. You might do it over the summer when you stop by your school library. The public librarian can help you get started. The directory of members at the Chamber of Commerce website will let you discover which ones are closest to you.

Once you know the small businesses, you can drop by. Wait until the owner/manage isn't busy with a customer. You don't want to interrupt their business. If you are asked if you need help and introduce yourself as the school librarian, wait until they are free. Then explain you want to know the community better and so are visiting local places of business.

Don't lead by speaking of the library. Ask them about the community, the best things and the ones they would like to see improve. You are trying to get a sense of who they are and whether they have a positive or negative mindset.

In your exploration of the community, talk to a real estate agent about the home market situation. You can also do some shopping when it is logical. As you walk around be open to opportunities to introduce yourself. Look into Kiwanis and Rotary to see what they are doing and whether they have any current projects.

All this helps you become *Confident* in knowing where to go and whom to ask when you are looking for funding to sponsor an activity at the library or find possible people who can contribute their expertise to a project you are doing.

Committed

Support your confidence by focusing on your "Why." Remember it is your "perspiration" and "motivation." What you do as you move outward takes work. It is a challenge that many librarians overlook. The days are already full, but the potential for what it could mean to how you and the library are seen in difficult times politically and for your budget are worth making the extra effort.

Parents

The issue of book challenges and banning makes it easy to regard parents as potential threats. Shift that mindset and recognize their potential for being library supporters. Several routes exist for making them advocates.

On conference evenings or when the administration has scheduled an open house, set up a colorful invitation for them to come to the library when they enter the building. Greet them when they arrive. Particularly if refreshments are not offered in the school lobby, have coffee and pastries for those who took you up on your invitation.

The teachers will have displays of the most recent student projects, so try to set up one using older student work to show what happens in the library. You might have a bulletin board with student "reviews" of the library. Prepare a floor plan showing the different areas of the library and where they are located. Have printouts for parents to take.

When there are only a few parents in the library, give "guided" tours to them. Point out your Mission and Vision Statements. Explain why it is important. Share your "Why." Your goal for the evening is for them to see you are *Committed* to giving your best to develop their child's ability to become a lifelong learner in an information-rich world.

If your library is genrefied, this is a good time to explain it to them and give them the reasons for it. If you have a makerspace, show it off, describing what students have used it to do and make. Give parents an opportunity to try making something of their own.

With your administrator's permission, sign up parents who are willing to volunteer in the library. Have a form where they can give their name, contact number, and availability. The benefits of parent volunteers are numerous.

Volunteers get to see your commitment in action. While working, they observe how and what you teach. They notice how you interact with students and create a safe welcoming environment for all of them. In becoming a part of the library, they develop a stake in its continuance and success.

They are there when you collaborate with teachers. It shows them how much the library impacts teaching and learning. The more they see, the more they become library advocates. At the same time, you are getting help with clerical tasks that normally take you away from your primary purpose.

As you get to know your parents better, you will discover their areas of expertise. You may be able to use their knowledge and abilities in a variety of ways. Someone with art ability might create bulletin boards. One who knows construction and is handy with tools could build a new display set up.

As volunteers become committed to the library, they will be willing to stand up for it. They will attend those critical board meetings. And their voices will be heard more quickly than yours.

Library Community

Your "Why" and that of the public librarian are similar. They, much like you, are the only one in the building. Yes, there are other librarians in the public library, but they are not focused on kids and teens. Look into what joint programming you can offer.

Look into the possibility of a combined author visit. Perhaps the author can come to the school at some point after lunch and visit a few classes, handing out bookmarks. They then can be at the public library after school. The kids will be even more excited and eager to attend that having already met the author.

The partnership you create by developing a working relationship with the public librarian strengthens both of you. Together you become a valuable presence in the community. You are both involved in their lives.

Chapter 1 discussed how your commitment, your "Why," is mirrored in many ways in the Mission and Vision Statements of the Professional Library Associations to which you belong. You have shared values with your whole library community. Review their statements to see how close they come to your own Mission and Vision. Incorporate words you like from them to tweak your own statements.

For example, on the AASL website you find its Mission, "The American Association of School Librarians empowers *Leaders* to transform teaching and learning." "Transform" speaks to being a *Change Agent*. This might add power to your statement. As mentioned in Chapter 1, its Vision is "Every school librarian is a *Leader*; every *Learner* has a school librarian." Your *state's school library association* probably has a Mission and Vision Statement. See to what extent it mirrors the AASL's statements.

The ALA Vision is, "Core members play a central role in every library, shaping the future of the profession by striking a balance between maintenance and innovation, process and progress, collaborating and leading." Collaborating is part of the 5 Cs and Leading is one of the 3 Ls.

ISTE's website says its Vision is "that all students engage in transformative learning experiences that spark their imagination and prepare them to thrive in learning and life." The word "transform" is here again.

The IST+ASCD website gives its Mission as "We empower educators to reimagine and redesign learning through impactful pedagogy and meaningful technology use. We achieve this by offering transformative professional learning, fostering vibrant communities, and ensuring that digital tools and experiences are accessible and effective." What words here resonate with you?

IFLA's Vision is Sustainable futures for all through knowledge and education. Its Core Values, abbreviated by me, include "endorsement of the principles of freedom of access to information, ideas and works of imagination; the belief that people, communities and organizations need universal and equitable access to information, ideas and works of imagination; the commitment to promote and value diversity and inclusion."

Business Community

You know your values, but which ones might you have in common with the local business community? You both want to create welcoming environments bringing people in. Use that when you visit them.

Comment on the way they welcome people. Continue by talking about the importance you place on making the library a safe, welcoming space for all. If the business isn't too busy at that time, go on with your conversation. Solicit their reaction to what you said.

Ask about their memories of the library when they were in school or before. Learn whether they use the public library. Why or why not? If they do use the public library, what is their purpose in going or accessing its online services?

Share your own childhood library memories, highlighting the many differences. Note that then, as now, it made you feel welcome. Did their childhood library do the same?

How has their business changed over time? Keeping up with the times is vital in business as it is for school libraries. Share any recent changes and any plans or hopes for future changes.

You won't discuss all of this in one visit. They have a business to run. When you feel you have used enough of their time, thank them for talking with you. Ask if they would mind if you come back some day and continue the conversation.

As with any relationship, it builds slowly. Look for opportunities to bring something of value to the business owner in your next visit.

In exploring the website of your local Chamber of Commerce look for a Vision and/or Mission Statement. It might say something about advancing the economic, industrial, professional, civic, and cultural welfare of the area and supporting those activities believed to be beneficial to the community and area. These will be values you can point to when you have a project that needs funding or extra hands.

Connected

Making connections is a crucial step in becoming an Involved School Librarian. You want to be known in the places that have influence.

Parents

We say our library is a safe, welcoming place for all. We direct it to our students and teachers, but we need to look for ways to make it a welcoming place for parents. You began building that connection by how you met them on conference and/or open house nights, but there is always more.

On those nights they saw a library without students. Although your displays captured some of what happens in the library, they still aren't likely to appreciate the range of teaching and services that come from the library. Look for opportunities to give them more information as to what students receive from an active library.

If there is a parent-teacher group, contact the leader and offer to do programs for them. It shouldn't be too long. They usually have something they want to discuss at their meeting. Those who don't have meetings might be willing to host one, in the library of course, and give you the time to do a longer presentation.

Ask them to consider becoming a parent volunteer in the library. If you have one in action you can talk about some ways the group has contributed to the library. Explain the time volunteers are expected to give. If you have any restrictions in place, such as not bringing younger children, be sure to mention them.

In an elementary school, you can talk about how to help their child choose a book at the public library. For upper grades you can do book talks about your most recent acquisitions or how research is done, explaining the database you have.

Point out that research sounds so easy these days with so much available on cell phones, but it is actually more complex. Speak about information literacy and some basic ways to avoid misinformation and disinformation. Let them know that it's part of the teaching you do as a librarian.

Highlight the school's website. Explain how they can access the library's page. Review areas they would find helpful. If you have a LibGuide for parents, this is an excellent opportunity to share it with them.

Library Community

Deepen your connection with the public library. We are stronger together and, as seen in Chapter 8, we have similar challenges. When we have built a solid relationship, we are better able to respond in difficult situations.

Invite the children's or youth/teen services librarian to your library. Have them bring any flyers for upcoming events and programs which you can distribute. Try and have several classes come to meet them. See if student projects can be displayed.

You have been on the AASL website when dealing with book challenges, now explore it to further connect to other school librarians nationally. Review the tabs along the top to see how being *Connected* to AASL gives you greater ability to make such a transformation in your school community.

See Best Digital Tools with award winners listed by year along with a description of what each provides. Advocacy provides Resources and Toolkits developed by AASL including the Crisis Toolkit and the School Library Program Health and Wellness Toolkit. Use the Get Involved tab to step out of your comfort zone and be a part of your transformation and that of other school librarians. The volunteer form allows you to identify how big or small a role you are ready to take on.

When you attend a library conference, whether state or national, make it a point to get to know other conference attendees.

The various meal functions are an opportunity to talk about what you and they are doing in your work and personal lives. Meeting someone face-to-face solidifies your contact. Exchange email addresses and possibly phone numbers. Expanding your PLN gives you access to more ideas and help.

Further expand your PLN by narrowing your focus. This is not a contradiction. It refers to becoming part of one or more of your association's sections. AASL has an Educators of School Librarians Section (ESLS) (to which I belong), an Independent Schools Section (ISS), and a Supervisors Section (SPVS).

If you haven't done so already, use Library and School Library social media. I have The School Librarian's Workshop (www.facebook.com/groups/57409801076). There is also Canva Librarians (www.facebook.com/groups/canvalibrariansandteachers) with Kristina Holzweiss as the administrator, Learning Librarians (www.facebook.com/groups/canvalibrariansandteachers), Librarians (www.facebook.com/groups/canvalibrariansandteachers), LM_Net Group (www.facebook.com/groups/canvalibrariansandteachers), and others. Find the ones you like and add them to your PLN.

BlueSky (https://bsky.social/about) is a relatively new social media outlet. It came into being as many became concerned about Twitter, now X. It's still in the growth stage but it is worth joining. It offers many ways to connect further with the school library community. It lets you follow school librarians or you can follow those librarians who regularly offer information that interests you.

Keep in mind the connection that IFLA offers. At some point you might want to become a librarian in another part of the world. IFLA gives you access to school librarians in your country of choice, learning more about what you might experience and challenges you might face.

Keep file of all the Resources for dealing with book challenges so you have them ready as needed. In addition to the ones already mentioned, also check the Book Résumés link on those pages that have them for any titles that have been challenged in your library. Additionally, consider the Office for Intellectual Freedom (OIF), Unite Against Book Bans, and Book Riot.

Business Community

You have met the people in your business community. They now know you as the school librarian. You want to maintain this connection. Use your PLN for ideas on how to keep that connection intact and growing. When the time comes, you will be able to gain their help for whatever appropriate project you have in mind.

Some of these community members might be parents of your students. On parent conference nights have a sign-in sheet for parents that includes a column for expertise and business owners in the area. You can honestly inform those who choose to fill in the form that you are gathering the information to find volunteers and sponsors to help with future library plans.

As an example, you might want to make some modifications in the library, such as repaint a wall. It is hard to get that included in a budget, but a local paint store might donate the paint and necessary brushes and clean up material. Volunteer parents can do the actual painting.

With administrator approval, bring in a local business owner to talk "shop" to a class or classes aligned with what they do. Your principal is likely to be supportive if you have clearly identified how it would support student learning, since it would also increase the likelihood of support for the school budget.

For those of you who work in a tech school, this is a logical connection. Going beyond the obvious, think of other possibilities. In making the connections with business owners, you have a wide range of areas which are their markets. You also have discovered which ones are most personable and which have or would be open to having interns from the high school.

Before the business owner comes, identify which classes would be the best ones for them to speak with. Talk with teachers before you set your plan in motion to ensure they are onboard with the mini event. Explain the purpose and get their input.

Teachers might also recommend students who are not currently in their class who would enjoy and benefit from it. Require those attending to submit questions in advance to ask the businessperson. Also find out if your speaker would be amenable to responding to questions students have for which there wasn't enough time to get to them, or if the question came up after they had time to reflect on what they learned.

Communicator

Now that you have connected with these members of your outside community, think of the messages you want to send them. Your knowledge of who they are and their knowledge of you will help you use the language most likely for them to receive it. Remember, communication does not rely only on words. It's your actions that make the words have meaning.

Parents

Aside from those parents who have a political agenda, the more you communicate with parents, the more likely they are to become allies and strong supporters. Set up a LibGuide for parents to keep them informed about the library.

If your school doesn't have LibGuides you will have to purchase your own from SpringShare (www.springshare.com/libguides). The cost depends on the size of your school. The good news is that as part of the purchase price, SpringShare will do the heavy lifting in designing your LibGuide.

Plan on what you want to feature on your LibGuide. Include information on how to keep their kids safe online. Identify databases with links to access them to sources such as Common-Sense Media. Consider the different parent needs depending on the level of their kids.

At the elementary level, have advice and resources to help parents promote their children's love and skills as readers. For middle and high school level provide information on ethical use of information. Give links on how to evaluate sources. Include the citation format used in your school. Address problems with AI use in research.

Here are some examples of categories to put in the LibGuide:

- Resources on Digital Safety
- Resources on Information Literacy

- Plagiarism
- Online Databases
- AASL Standards
- Studies on the value of School Librarians.

Post a photo of you as a way for them to see and recognize you. Give your email allowing them to contact you and ask questions. You might want to set a time frame for those questions as you won't necessarily have time to check for emails from parents during school hours.

You don't want the LibGuide to become static. Plan on updating it every so often. Highlight library "happenings." Show a project students completed and what the learning outcome was. Avoid pictures that would identify students.

Once you have created your LibGuide be sure to inform parents that it exists and how to access it. Let them know what is included in the LibGuide. Making this connection creates a greater awareness of what the library contributes to student learning. As they use it, parents become more involved with the school library and recognize their need to support it.

Library Community

Your library is in continuous communication. From emails to webinars and conferences, this is your source to what is happening in libraries, whether on the local, state, or national level. Keep track of what is happening. The knowledge will enable you to keep your library program fresh and allow you to know if you need to pivot.

Celebrate good news and learn how to incorporate the success into your own practice. The information gives you a wider perspective and an awareness about potential problems. With the forewarning, you have time to prepare and access resources that will help.

In your LibGuide, consider posting information about activities and events at the public library. Arrange to have library and possibly school events publicized at the public library. Your connection builds with this two-way communication.

Volunteer to serve on a committee of your School Library Association and possibly chairing it. You will be communicating with the members and growing as an Involved School Librarian. Run for an office. It requires moving out of your comfort zone but recognize the benefits of getting a better understanding of the strengths and weaknesses of the association.

The next step in leaving your comfort zone is to move up to the national level. Again start with a committee. When you finish on one, look to another that interests you. At some point, you might be ready to run for an office.

Those of you who are really venturesome can perhaps attend an IFLA World Library and Information Congress (WLIC). This is a conference with a global scope. It does offer some virtual elements.

As you increase the scope of your service to the library community, your skills as a *Communicator* will grow. Although you will be communicating widely, your experience will improve how you communicate with teachers and administrators in your school community. Your message will be clearer and more focused.

What you give is returned to you. Your *Confidence* continues to grow. Your *Commitment* is obvious and enhanced. The widened *Connections* increase your knowledge, opening the way to grow your library, benefitting your school community.

Business Community

You now have made inroads into the business community. Look for ways to increase your connection to it. It doesn't have to be huge, but little by little it can build.

Share what is happening in the school. Business owners might be aware of how the high school sports team is doing but rarely know more. However, they do vote. The school budget affects them directly. You want them to see the value of what is going on in your school.

Ask if they have children in the school. Encourage those who do attend back-to-school nights to visit the library. Talk about special happenings that have occurred or are in the planning stage.

If you are at the high school level, think of those businesses which would be of interest to students. You might have them talk to students about their business, what they take pride in and what challenges they face. A music store owner can speak with a music class. A computer store owner is a natural to meet with a STEM class.

The owners/managers might take or be willing to have student interns. Work with the guidance counselor on how to go about making it happen. Do inform your administrator, of course.

Change Agent

You have established a relationship with those who are your outside communities. The first 4 Cs have given you the foundation to make changes. As an Involved School Librarian, you now turn to these groups and work with them to make the changes needed for the library to thrive.

Parents

The best way to deal with challenges is to have laid the groundwork so they don't occur. You want parents to see you as their partner in helping their children reach their fullest potential. You also want parents to be your partner in promoting the value of the library program.

If their children are on your library council or if they are parent volunteers, you have a core from which to draw on. Keep track of school board meetings. You particularly want to go to ones where you know book banning will be a topic.

Their attendance becomes extremely important if your district becomes embroiled in book banning. Provide information to assist those who are attending. It's a good idea to attend yourself, but the voice of parents will be heard more strongly.

When planning changes for the library, use your LibGuide to keep parents informed. Explain why the change will improve learning. Seek their help with any aspects of the change they can help with.

You might even share Ranganathan's fifth law of library science, "The Library Is a Growing Organism" (see Chapter 1). Remind them of how much libraries have changed since they were students and why it was necessary to change. Making happenings in the library transparent to them brings the library into their lives.

Library Community

Change is a constant in the library community. Those not involved in education change jobs with greater frequency. Tenure tends to keep school librarians – and teachers – in place. Administrator turnover happens far more often.

Your relationship with the public librarian will give you early warning if there is to be a personnel change there. Meet the new person as soon as possible. If there is to be a new director make a connection with that person.

Your School Library Associations change officers every year. You may be one of them. They also form new committees as needed, launch new initiatives, and offer new resources on their webpage. The national ones do so as well.

The changes may be in support of school libraries and librarians. You might want to be a part of this larger effort. It will take a greater use of your time. Balance new commitments with what time you need for your school community and your personal life.

Build self-care into your new obligations. Physical and mental burnout will not help you achieve your goals. Take care of yourself to make changes possible.

Business Community

You aren't a *Change Agent* in the business community, but change happens in that community. Stores close and other ones open. Just as when you have a new administrator, you need to establish a connection with the recent opening.

As the first business posts indications of closing, find out if those leaving know anything about the newcomer. Keep an eye on the location as it undergoes the changes to prepare for the incoming business. You might have an early opportunity to speak with the owner/manager as it is occurring. Follow up with the connection once it's established.

While connections are what you are making, the importance is to recognize and utilize them to promote the library program. By involving yourself in the local business, you are creating ways for them to become involved with the library.

As you read through the recommendations for how you interact with the business community, you are probably and logically thinking you don't have time for it. The truth is you don't have much. What has been presented are possibilities to keep in mind and utilize when you can. You can always use a new supporter.

You have now seen the vast outside community in which you can interact. How far you go with each depends on your priorities, interests, and time. Start small and work your way outwards.

10

The 5 Ps in Action

Discover how being *Passionate, Purposeful, Planner, Professional,* and *Powerful* combine with what you have learned from the 5 Cs to make you a fully Involved School Librarian. Reaching people's emotions creates stronger relationship. Your emotional attributes will involve you more firmly in their thinking and actions.

Passionate

Parents

You and parents share a passion. The students are the center of why you do what you do. Just like you, they want their kids to get the best possible education and be prepared for their unknowable future. The challenge for you is to use your ability as a *Communicator* to make them aware of what you do.

When students achieve something as part of their library experience, send a message home. You can use email or write your message and send it home with the student. Prepare the format in advance. Consider what parents might like to hear.

Use language the parents will understand. We are so accustomed to educational jargon, we tend to use it without thinking about it. "Learning experience" is a blurry phrase to them. You might say, "Joe did an exemplary job researching the effect of humans on the climate." Be as specific as possible.

DOI: 10.4324/9781003647058-14

It's not only skills but behaviors that you can commend. For example, you could inform parents that their child was extremely supportive of another student as they worked together on their assignment. The idea is to show that you and the parent are in this together. It is showing them that you care and "see" their kid.

If you have parent volunteers, every day they come to work in the library is an opportunity to show your passion for what you do, and what they are helping you do. On a smaller scale, seek parent volunteers when you hold a book fair. They volunteered their time in part because they are curious about the library and possibly about you.

Beginning as they help you set the fair up, you are "on.' Let them see what you know without you bragging about it. Show your passion as you greet and deal with students individually as classes come in to make selections. They get to see how you guide students to the books you know they will enjoy based on your experiences with them.

Library Community

You have recognized your shared commitment with the other members of the library community. In the same way, you share the same passion. You serve different types of patrons, bring different expertise to your work, but for the most part you are all *Passionate* about what you do.

You and the public librarian have the same students in common. Although you see more students, they get a different perspective. The ones who come to the library after school are not under the time and other constraints of their academic environment. Seek to discover which kids the librarian sees often enough to know. Share with each other what you have learned.

If the library holds an after-school program, try to visit it. Younger kids might even be surprised you exist outside the school building. When it's appropriate and with the librarian's permission given ahead of time, join in.

Younger children are usually brought to the public library by their parents. Meeting them in a different setting gives you a broader picture of who they are. Take the opportunity to engage them in conversation.

Are they readers? What are their favorite genres? If you share the interest, mention the author and book you are reading. If you don't normally read in that genre, ask for a recommendation and say you will try one. Mean what you say by reading the book and sending the parent a message about it.

Bring your passion to your State Library Association. You have made some level of commitment to it, now participate in what touches your emotions. Review the committees to find the one or ones that do that.

Some of you are *Passionate* about intellectual freedom. Others feel strongly about promoting school librarians. If you belong to related associations such as being an AASL and an ISTE member, you may care about strengthening the ties. In that case, seek to become a liaison from one to the other.

Business Community

Owners of small businesses and sometimes the managers are often *Passionate* about what they do. In your interactions with them look for evidence of their passion. Comment upon it and share that you also feel *Passionate* about what you do. Learning that you feel as strongly about your life's work as they do creates an understanding of what impels you to improve it.

Talk about how their love for what they do has helped their business grow. Respond to what they say by speaking about how you build readers and young people ready to be successful in wherever direction their future path takes them.

With this emotional level of connection between the businessperson and you, you can reach out to them as needed. You might ask them to sponsor a special event in the library. It will also help their business as you will acknowledge their contribution. Their particular business might be in a position to help you with an aspect of library renovation or some other project.

Purposeful

Parents

Back-to-school and parent conference nights are opportunities to share your Mission and its importance to the growth and learning of students. Talk to them about what they want their kids to get from what they learn in school. Respond by sharing how the library contributes to that. Give examples and point out any relevant display of student work.

You want them to feel that your passion for working with students is one you share with the parents' hopes and dreams for their children's future. Communicating the importance of your Mission Statement to parents increases the emotional connection you are building. Whether you do so directly or indirectly, bring it to your relations with them. Speak to your shared interest in their kids' success.

Point to ways you make the library a safe and welcoming space for all. Discuss any modifications you have made to address accommodations for special needs students that sends that welcoming message. Although in some communities you might want to be careful about it, this is a good time to have a display of books reflecting diversity.

If you have a LibGuide, find out how many parents have accessed it. Remind them of what resources it offers. Ask them if they want other information included. All this reinforces your willingness to work with them in furthering their children's growth.

Whether or not you have a LibGuide, remind them they can reach you by phone or email. Add the caveat that you might not be able to respond immediately, as students always come first in your attention. When your actions prove the truth of your words, they will see that you are serious in being partners with them in wanting the best for their children.

Library Community

In serving the same community of students, you and the public librarian not only share core values, but you also both know what you want to accomplish and why it is important. It is why you can willingly share information on each other's projects. The benefits to both of your specific communities is obvious.

At the state level, being *Passionate* and *Purposeful* are the driving force for advocacy initiatives. You call your representatives and send the letters, knowing that together you are stronger. You make time in your busy life to serve on committees.

You purpose is a compelling motivation to participate at the national level. It takes time and money to attend conferences, but you seek time to connect with other librarians. You gather strength and are empowered by the presentations. The social connections you make during conferences remind you that you are not alone.

Business Community

While becoming involved in the business community isn't one of your primary focuses, including it can be done in the small steps previously discussed. And the rewards will show up in the voting booth as well as help with some of your projects. Your purpose will help you to keep making inroads.

Amelia Earhart said, "The most difficult thing is the decision to act. The rest is merely tenacity." I remind myself that the hardest part of exercise is putting your sneakers on. It's the Newtonian concept of a body at rest and a body in motion. Once you get started it's easier to continue.

The one thing business owners are passionate about is growing their business. In Chapter 9 we discussed making contact with them and noted they can be a source of help with various projects. You have engaged with their passion, developing an emotional bond. It's not a huge thing, but it's there underneath the talk.

When you are planning a project and can use their aid, take time to prepare your Ask. Acknowledge and/or compliment how much their caring for what they do shows in the way they conduct business and even the atmosphere they have created to welcome their customers. Share how you work to create a welcoming environment for the library.

That conversation would be an excellent segue for a renovation project. With a few more tweaks it can work for sponsoring an author visit. Consider briefly referring to the author's message or whatever connection you can make. Point out that you would be giving the business credit for what they have done. You would also include that information in the channel you use to communicate with parents who are current or future customers.

The idea is to use infrequent visits to develop recognition of who you are. When the time comes to ask for help, you won't be a stranger.

Planner

Planning requires a combination of skills. You need to know clearly what your goal is. You should be able to connect it to your Vision and Mission. Being *Confident* is needed to believe you can achieve the results you want. A timeline keeps you on track, and you have built in assessments at key places in your plan.

Parents

Your interactions with parents don't usually require a formal plan such as the one explained but keep the component concepts in mind when you are seeing a group of parents. For a back-to-school night you should know your targeted result for the evening.

For a presentation you might be giving at a parent-teacher group, a more specific plan is needed. The first part is choosing the topic. Choose one that has a strong connection to them. Keeping kids digitally safe at home is one possibility. Showing them how to access the library's online databases at home is another option.

Know your time frame. In the first instance, you will introduce ways to verify sources. To help them retain the information, you might give them some of the examples you use with students and have them verify the sources. If you are doing the second idea, you will need to allow time for parents to try using the databases while they are in the library. No matter what your topic is, you do need to have time for questions. Your goal for the night is for parents to recognize the value of the library to their child's success and further your partnership with them.

Library Community

When you plan to have an event such as an author visit, or are working on a renovation project, include the public librarian as a step in the process. The upcoming author visit can be publicized at the library. They can display a poster you create along with how to sign up to volunteer as needed or sponsor part of the event.

For the renovation project, the public library is a source for ideas since they are associated with the Chamber of Commerce. Many of their patrons are the local business owners. Share your plans and seek their input. Just as librarians know the just-right book for someone, they might be able to point you to the just-right business owner to support your plan.

Your PLN is your source for what other librarians have planned and what they have achieved. You can find out how they have connected with their business community for what results. You can follow up as needed to get more information.

Business Community

Speak to the business owner(s) you have targeted as being likely sources of help. Let them know you believe it will be mutually beneficial. Explain, since you want to give them the big picture showing how they fit in and where it will serve their business interests, you would like to set up a time when you could meet. This is after you have paid a few visits to introduce yourself.

On the appointed time, bring your completed, polished plan on your laptop so you can easily display it as you explain what and why you are planning. Your PowerPoint or preferred tool for presentation should have the formal plan with your goal, steps with any needs for doing it, and assessment for key steps and at completion. Include when and where any funding is required.

Let the business owner look at the plan while you talk. Don't read it – they are doing that. This is the time for you to bring your passion and purpose to the plan. The emotion is what sells. Finish up by highlighting how you will be publicly thanking the business owner for their help. Add your belief that it will drive customers to their business.

Professional

Remember, the importance of this attribute is not the fact that librarianship is a profession with all that entails. Being seen as a

Professional is about your presence. Your presence is what you display. It is how people see you. You create it with your poise and your ability to make things happen.

Parents

You want parents to trust you with their children. In today's climate, that has become more important than ever. Having them see you as a *Professional* is crucial to creating their trust in you.

How you communicate with parents is foundational to creating the trust. Whether you use a LibGuide or other tool, the look of the tool as much as the content sends a strong message. It should show you know what you are doing and keep up with current needs and developments.

On back-to-school and parent conference evenings, your look is part of the package you present. Your dress counts, as does your demeanor. You are not a know-it-all and don't use a lot of educational jargon to impress them. You want them to see you as a seeker and finder of needed information. You welcome their partnership in their child's growth.

There may be times when you meet parents outside of school, particularly if you live in the community. You do want to engage in friendly conversation with them. Keep the talk related either to their child or to something you are doing. Never discuss another student or speak negatively about a teacher or administrator.

Library Community

Here you are a *Professional* among professionals. These are your peers. Look to the ones who embody the concept of *Professional*. Learn how they do it by consciously being attuned to how they present themselves.

Use the resources offered through your membership to further develop your *Professional* knowledge and skills. Look for opportunities to earn micro-credentials which are becoming more well-known. Inform your administrator when you earn them.

Finding a mentor is another way to grow your presence as a *Professional*. Identify what you seek to accomplish and look for someone who does it well. Ask them to mentor you. Should someone ask you to be their mentor, determine what they are looking to learn. Also establish guidelines for how and when you will communicate with each other.

State and National Library Associations offer awards and grants. Explore what is available. Apply for one that is closest to your expertise and need. The process of applying for it will grow your knowledge and understanding. Winning it will increase the perception of others, particularly your administrators, as to your level of professionalism.

Business Community

When you go into the *Business Community*, you are the face of the school library. They have read the news. There are those who have developed a negative view of you and the library as a result. Your interactions with them can cause them to see what you do in a positive light.

In your conversations with them, be mindful as to how you react to what you might easily see as accusations. Avoid becoming argumentative or hostile in response. Keeping a calm demeanor will help you send the message that you are a *Professional*.

If the businessperson levels a charge about what you are doing to children, be careful not to deny it with a negative. I learned in a media training that the human brain will skip over the negative and keep the rest. It sounds weird, but rather than say, "School librarians don't teach children to become gay," state what librarians do. Your response might be something like, "School librarians seek to make the library a safe and welcoming space for all."

Stay with the positives. At appropriate points you can ask them questions. For example, if you responded about the environment you try to create in the library, ask them how their school library made them feel. If possible, you want to create that emotional connection they have to their school library experience.

Powerful

When stepping outside your school community with the intention of building wider support for the library, you need to bring your power. You have learned that power comes in several forms, now use it as you become involved in the community.

Parents

You have been using Power With in your interactions with parents. You continually highlight your shared interest. You both want the best for their children.

Power With is the basis for building relationships and you do want parents to feel they have a relationship with you. The relationship makes them want the library to continue to grow and improve the program and services it delivers to their children. Power With is a strong force for creating advocates.

You also want to use your Expert Power. As parents get to know you, they discover how much you know and why it is valuable to them as well as their children. What you said during those back-to-school and parent conference nights began their awareness of your expertise. Any program you gave for the parent-teacher group added to it. Your LibGuide and/or other communication channel you use to connect with them solidified it.

Parents have a lot of power. They have Legal Power as a parent. They have control over their children. They can reward or punish them. Parents also have Expert Power. They do know their children, although some are better at that than others. Be open to hearing what they might tell you about their children.

Once you have built a relationship with parents, you can use your Power To. If you have parent volunteers, they would be a good place to start. Power To addresses the strength of the individual in creating the world they live in. None of us can choose what happens to us. We all have a choice in how we deal with it.

Power To says one person can change the world. We know how Rachel Carson alerted us to human caused environmental damage in her book *Silent Spring*. Greta Thunberg went from a personal school strike to arousing world-wide concern about climate change.

You aren't trying to incite a global rejection of book banning and attacks on librarians, although there are efforts to reach that goal. You want parents to attend board meetings when the library and its collection are likely to be targeted. Their voices are louder than yours. The more parents are present and standing up for the importance of school libraries and librarians the greater the likelihood they will be heard.

Library Community

Your home community is rooted in Power With. The differences in which community you serve or where you work are minor compared with the shared values you have in common. The bond unites you when libraries and librarians are threatened. You recognize and understand that together you are stronger.

You and your public librarian need to keep each other informed about any indications of a potential or actual issue that warrants a combined response. We have seen that when the school library is attacked the challenge can spread to the public library. Forewarned is forearmed.

Your State School Library Association usually has a link where you can alert them when you and your library come under fire. It usually has resources you can access for information on the best way to proceed. There are likely to be links to ALA resources.

It's important to report challenges so the library community is aware of them and can respond and/or provide help. If links for reporting are not on your State Library Association's website, you can find them at ALA's Report Censorship Page. It includes links for the specific challenge and allows for anonymous reporting.

Power To is a reminder that you can make a difference along with the other members of the library community by supporting and helping to grow the resources available for librarians when they face challenges. The State and National Library Associations need people to serve on committees such as those on Advocacy and Intellectual Freedom. By volunteering to be a member of one of those committees, you become part of the solution.

Stay informed on happenings throughout the country and even the world through your PLN. The library-related social media lets you know what different librarians are experiencing. Here is where you will learn how a librarian reacted to a challenge or another issue. You might be following it as it occurs.

Although it doesn't quite meet the description of Expert Power, knowledge is a power. Discover those librarians who took a strong stand against those targeting them. Learn what happened next. Identify with the fear and concern of others as well as what support they are given by others.

Although challenges are ever present, even in less politically charged time, there are other occasions where you draw on your power in the library community. When you are ready to seek a leadership position you need your Power Within. You have the confidence and belief in yourself to step out of your comfort zone.

Business Community

You are using your Power Within every time you take the risk of reaching out to the business community to support the library in some way. You have also used Power With as you brought your common feelings about what you both do and formed a connection. It isn't a deep connection but it is one that can help in gaining their backing for a project.

A power that isn't mentioned often is Charismatic Power, sometimes called Referent Power. It's the power that makes you like someone the first time you met them. Picture the people in your life. Think of the ones you just like to be with. There is something about them that invites you in.

Charismatic Power is inherent in the person's body language. Their smile and the rest of their face. The way they hold their arms. How they stand when talking to you. These elements all send the message that they are someone you would like to be with.

Combined with Power Within, it is potent power to strengthen your connection with businesspersons. When you walk into their store or office, you want them to smile and be obviously glad to see you. There is an inherent trust. That trust combined with your *Professional* presence incline them to become part of whatever project you propose.

Your Power Within will also help if you are dealing with attempts to censor and ban library material. In your conversations you can start by sharing your strong commitment to intellectual freedom and the importance of the library being a safe space for all. The board doesn't want to create problems for business owners. If they show up at a board meeting, their concerns will likely be heard.

In talking with business owners, mention that studies show strong school libraries make stronger schools. Add that they know that good schools bring business to a neighborhood that has them. People choose to live in neighborhoods with good schools and businesses nearby.

Once again, you are telling them, you are in this together. And together you are stronger. From being *Passionate*, *Purposeful*, and a *Planner* along with your *Professional* presence, you have built relationships with parents, gained knowledge and support for your endeavors from the library community, and found a place for the library in the business community. You are an Involved School Librarian.

11

The 3 Ls in Action

The 3 Ls are like breathing. The first two, *Listener* and *Learner*, are what you inhale. The third, *Leader*, is what you exhale. It brings everything together to make you the strongest possible *Leader*, one who is involved in all your communities.

Listener

Active listening is not simply hearing what the other person is saying. Your body language is sending a message showing you are fully listening. Be alert to their body language as well, since it is telling you if they are talking about something that really concerns them.

Parents

You see almost all the students. You have contact with far fewer parents. Make those meetings count.

At those back-to-school and conference nights, include time for them to ask you questions and talk about their kids. Certainly, when you give a presentation for the parent-teacher group, you will have a place for questions. When you are talking to a few or more parents at one time, remind them of how they can reach you if they have some personal questions and concerns. Your LibGuide or other communication channel does have a link for them to email you.

Parent volunteers, whether they are there as part of an event such as a book fair or are regularly scheduled to do library work, are a source of information when you actively listen. When they speak of their child, you may find out something that will let you know how better to meet that child's need.

Parents also see the library with different eyes. You walk in every day. It is your home. It's familiar as it is and so you don't see beyond the surface. Encourage your volunteers to let you know when they see something that doesn't seem right. They might alert you to little things like labels that seem confusing or even a spelling error in a display.

Thanking them and showing you made the change as result of what they said tells them that you listen to them. When they see you as an active *Listener* it increases their positive feelings about the library.

When you tune into parents, you are likely to overhear their gossip. They talk about teachers, positively or negatively. They also talk about other parents.

You never join in the gossip. If parents talk to you directly about teachers or other parents, you only respond if what they say is positive. When they make disparaging comments, say you appreciate them being willing to share their feelings. But make it clear to them that you don't engage in negative conversations about the teachers, administrators, or other parents. If their issue is with a teacher, suggest they set up a meeting with the teacher. Remember, the library is a safe space for *all*.

Library Community

Tune into what is happening in your library community. When speaking with your public librarian, find out what people are happy about or what is getting them upset. They are likely to hear these things before you do. The concerns and emotions swirling around could extend into the school community.

AASL has e-Newsletters (www.ala.org/aasl/pubs/enews) that give you a snapshot into some current focuses. ALA Connect sends emails with a list of different topics that have arisen. Responses are shown with pertinent links.

Podcasts are another means of listening to what the library community has to say. While not my preferred method of listening or learning, as I have trouble focusing on what I am hearing without seeing anything, I usually end up playing solitaire on my computer while listening.

ISTE offers a number of podcasts for members (https://iste.org/learning-library/podcasts). This is a good source for the latest information on edtech. There are podcasts on AI that will give you a better sense of where and how to use it. They will also give you information to share with teachers and administrators on where to incorporate AI and where caution is needed.

ASCD is an additional source of podcasts (www.ascd.org/podcasts). As the Association for Supervisors and Curriculum Developers, the topics of the workshops are targeted to them. Among the subjects are leadership, classroom management, and school culture. You are a *Leader* and will find many of its podcasts beneficial.

Look online for more suggestions of podcasts. You might want to join Podyssey for The Eight Best Podcasts for School Librarians (https://podyssey.fm/curated-podcasts/id2955-best-podcasts-for-school-librarians).

Hopefully, you attend your State and National School Library Conferences where you have the opportunity to listen to the many speakers on diverse topics. At conferences, you also meet informally with other librarians. You know a number of them and will meet more while there.

Over a meal, as you encounter them in the exhibit hall, or while waiting for a program to begin, listen to what they have to say. Hear what they have to say about successes as well as issues of concern. These planned or spontaneous encounters give you an opportunity to get support for one of your problems or an idea for something new.

Business Community

You don't have to visit the various businesses to listen. Be mindful of how your students and parent volunteers talk about the owners and managers of these businesses. If you live in the community, you have your own views of some of them. Any of your teachers may mention a local business.

It doesn't mean that all these comments are accurate. It's just something to add to your knowledge about those places and people. Eventually you will be able to corroborate or dismiss the remarks.

When you do go out into the community, continue to actively listen. Wandering around a store while waiting to approach the owner or other worker as you have been doing, listen for how they speak with potential customers. Are they brusque or attentive? Are they only going for a sale or listening for the customer's needs?

You can also listen to how they speak with male and female customers. Is it the same? Do they assume women know less? If the business place is more natural for a woman, do they immediately try to help the man out?

In speaking with anyone who works there, note the way they speak to you. Is it similar to what you have heard them speak with their customers?

If there are several employees, listen for how they speak with each other. Is there a sense of camaraderie and mutual support or does it sound competitive? If the owner or manager is present how do they speak to the other workers?

As previously noted, although the business community can become library advocates and supporters, this is not your primary focus. Your time is limited. All this listening won't be happening often. This section is meant to raise your awareness when you do have time and are out in the community.

Learner

Continue "inhaling" the information you need. Although similar, this puts learning into hyper drive, giving it focus. It is separated from listening to help you become aware of the distinction between the two attributes and see how they each function. Not all listening results in learning. Not all learning is the result of listening. But when the two come together, you have something substantive that will guide you in your leadership and further you as an Involved School Librarian.

Put your listening into use. What have you learned? To what purpose?

Parents

During the back-to-school and parent conference nights, you might have heard them talk about their child. Whether they referred to a struggle, a preference, or bullying behavior by another kid, you now have information. Find out how valid their comments were.

Make a point of identifying the students' named. Observe how they behave with you, their teachers, and their peers. Does it fit?

Based on what you have learned about the students in question, adjust your behavior accordingly. Does the student need more attention from you? Keep an eye on the one you have discovered is a bully. Intercede when necessary and be aware of what they are doing when in the stacks.

Your parent volunteers may have spoken to you about things in the library that they see with their fresh eyes that should be changed. Sometimes these are little problems that can be easily fixed. When done, make sure to let the parent know you made the change.

If the issue is less easily managed, such as getting wheels on tables or moving sections of books to other locations, use your ability as a *Change Agent*. Do some strategic planning. Is it a matter of time or money?

When it's a matter of time, do you need to do it by yourself? If you can do it better and faster with help, who do you need to get to help?

Changes requiring money are generally more challenging. Much depends on how much money is needed. Check the grants and awards from your State and National Associations to see if possibilities exist there.

Getting budgetary funding has always been difficult. Now it comes close to impossible. DonorsChoose is a frequent go-to source. If you choose that route, work on your campaign carefully.

Your PLN might give you advice on how best to frame and sell your request. Your parents might participate if you inform them. And of course, always let your administrator know what you are planning and why.

Library Community

Among the podcasts you have listened to and the webinars you have attended, are there any that captured your attention as something you want to do? You are a *Planner*. When are you going to put the idea in motion? What is the best way to frame it? Who do you need to help with this?

If it is a large undertaking, develop a strategic plan to make it a reality. Since you know the podcaster or webinar presenters who gave you the information, you can contact them for help and advice. When you have incorporated it successfully into your library, thank the podcaster or presenter. They appreciate knowing they made a difference.

A conversation with your public librarian may have alerted you to a potential upcoming issue affecting the school library. Perhaps people are upset with the school budget and many plan to vote it down. Rising concern about the school library giving children "inappropriate" books means the next board meeting will be hearing from organized groups and individuals.

For the first possibility, review your probable budget request. Don't do any cutting now as what you submit will be the base for how much will be cut. Do your best to identify what you can cut or reduce that will incur the least damage to teaching and learning in the library.

For example, you will want to keep access to your databases. Be prepared to explain how much is lost if they are cut. Can your makerspace keep going with fewer additions and supplies? If you have magazine subscriptions, you might be able to drop them, figuring that your databases will fill in the holes.

Query your PLN for suggestions on how to manage budget cuts. There are plenty of librarians who have experienced it. Some of their solutions might help you.

When book challenges are surfacing, look for those parents who are likely to support you and the library. Hopefully, they will attend any board meetings when the issue will be raised. If you know who plans to go, support them with information to have in advance.

Give parents your Mission Statement to bring to the meeting. Discuss it with them so they can refer to it when they explain what the school library does and why it is so important. Listen (back to that) for any examples or experiences they can share based on what they have seen or learned.

The State and National Library Associations have resources to help you plan for this possibility. If you haven't planned in advance, there are also resources to deal with it as it happens. Of course being well prepared yields the best possible results. Your advocacy efforts with parents and the business community has hopefully developed supporters.

Business Community

You have listened to what parents have said about different businesses in the community. You have heard what the public librarian has said. They have let you know about the ones they consider helpful and outstanding. You have also heard about those that can be curt, somewhat judgmental, or even biased.

Some may have commented on one or two that are not trustworthy. If you are so inclined, you can check the Better Business Bureau and do a search using your zip code and the type of business to see their rating. Many are not rated. You can also see if the Federal Trade Commission has recorded any violations.

In your own conversations with the local business owners and managers you have learned which ones are *Passionate* about what they do. You have a sense of how well they are integrated into the community. You possibly have been brushed aside by a few because you weren't there to make a purchase.

When you are looking for help with a project, such as needing some bins, wheels put on tables, or a library remodel, you now are fairly certain who will be most likely to contribute. By now, they know who you are, but you will need to sell to get a buy-in. As always, before seeing the person you hope will support your project, speak with your principal. Explain what you are planning to do and why.

Talking with your administrator will help you refine your Ask when you do make your request. Take time to prepare it carefully. Be up front about what you want right away and say it will be a win for the business as well as the library. Immediately follow it up with specifics as to how it will benefit the business.

Whatever the project is, if at all appropriate, such as an author visit or the renovation project, inform the local newspaper so they can cover it. The article and photos will mention the local businessperson who supported it. Keeping your word builds the trust for getting future help. The coverage will also encourage different business people to participate in your next project.

Detailing all the steps makes this sound as though you are spending a lot of time in the business community. You don't have that time. Do it selectively. Keep it in the back of your mind so you don't forget they are there. As an Involved School Libarian you recognize businesses can be a help or an obstacle to the success of the library program.

Leader

We have arrived once again at the final attribute necessary to become a fully Involved School Librarian. Chapter 1 used this definition of "involved," as being "actively participating in something." You have discovered ways of actively participating in your school and the business communities, now see how being a *Leader* makes it all happen.

Vocabulary.com gives the definition of a Leader as being "the one in the charge, the person who convinces other people to follow." It further notes that a "great *Leader* inspires confidence in other people and moves them to action."[1]

You aren't always the one officially in charge, but you are *Confident* and inspire it in others. You know about the different types of Power and can access your power to convince others to follow your lead and take action.

Parents

Parents are the emotional core of your leadership in the outside community. They are invested in the success of their children. The 5 Cs, 5 Ps, and the first 2 Ls have formed the foundation for them to trust you are equally invested and involved in their children's success.

Actions speak louder than words, but the words you have spoken, combined with seeing those words in action, convince them. They have seen your passion and purpose in creating a library program that prepares students to be successful in their future.

Through the communication channels you have established, parents know what you are planning and feel the partnership you have fostered with them. They know how to reach you, experiencing the truth of your Mission Statement, seeing that the library does welcome everyone – including them.

Beyond knowing your plans, in many cases they have contributed to them. They have volunteered to help you with book fairs and may be giving scheduled help in the library. The parents have been a source of information for you about businesses in the community.

The parents' appreciation for the school library has undoubtedly led many to share their views with family and friends, extending the number of library supporters. If it proved necessary in your community, some have attended contentious board meetings, speaking in support of the library.

You have thanked them for the successes you have achieved together.

Library Community

Your leadership with the public librarian is a collaborative leadership. You each have plans that may need help from one another to carry out. Often the plans will benefit if you publicize theirs and they publicize yours. When crises such as book banning erupt, you stand together, helping each other get through it.

In your social network PLNs, you are a *Leader* when you organize a chat on a topic or bring relevant information to other members. Curating articles you share with them is Servant Leadership. It strengthens their connection with you.

As you become known for the articles you have shared, others in the PLN will bring questions and concerns to you. They will also share additional information they find on the subject. The more you know, the more you grow.

You show up as a *Leader* in your State and National School Library Associations when you chair committees or run for an office. Putting yourself in the spotlight that way takes Confidence and the willingness to step out of your comfort zone.

As a committee chair you oversee the direction the committee takes to serve the library community. You guide it to ensure that it does not get locked into doing only the tried and true but grows with the times.

You are unquestionably a *Leader* when you step up for an office, particularly to become the president of your state and possibly even your National Association. When you take on that position, you will need all 5 Cs, 5 Ps, and the other 2 Ls to bring your association forward. Taking on such a large job has always required the best you have to give. With today's challenging political climate, the demands are greater than ever.

Because you are *Confident* in the face of the demands of the position, you need to trust yourself to succeed and accept that you will make mistakes. Your Connections will minimize potential missteps. Being *Committed* will keep you going. You will be using your ability as a *Communicator* when you are being a *Change Agent*, addressing major issues of concern to school librarians.

To keep your energy flowing as you deal with the heavy responsibilities and duties that come with your position, you rely on being *Passionate* and *Purposeful*. Your *Professional* presence is a requirement in interactions which can be contentious. Careful Planning is essential, as is using the various types of power for you to be successful.

Listening and Learning is incorporated into your days. You can never know too much, since so much is at stake. Most of you are not contemplating running for an office, but as you incorporate all of the attributes discussed you will be growing as a *Leader*.

One day, you may surprise yourself and decide to take on the challenge of leading your State or National Library Association. Others have done it. You can as well. While that may never happen, what you have learned will make you a better *Leader* in your school library and in other areas of your life.

Business Community

Your first thought on starting this section was probably, you can't be a *Leader* in the business community. As surprising as it may sound, that was the whole purpose of your becoming involved in the community. What you are being is "the person who convinces other people to follow."

In your interactions with them, you have built a level of relationship with the ones who have participated in assisting you in some way. When you help someone, you become a participant in their success. You are likely to continue to support them.

When these business people show up for you, others in the community have some understanding of who you are. They have met you and learned of your passion and purpose. They have a sense of what you are committed to.

If and when the library is threatened either by budget cuts or book bans, the other business owners will recognize why the library is being defended. While they probably won't join your supporters, they won't be among the ones who want or are willing to be part of its demise. Keeping the numbers of those in opposition to the library low will lower their impact.

Coupled with your vocal supporters, you have a strong chance of keeping the library intact even if somewhat wounded. It then gives you a chance to make it even stronger as you regroup. What you have done is created a climate for sustainability.

Sustainability is not only for the environment. It is for anything that is likely to face challenges to its continued existence. By being a fully Involved School Librarian, you have created the likelihood that you and the library will continue, despite any storms that may come.

You have now discovered how integrating all the attributes (*Confident, Committed, Connected, Communicator, Change Agent,*

Passionate, Purposeful, Planner, Professional, Powerful, Listener, Learner, and *Leader*) has brought you to where you have the tools to shape your own environment and continue to deliver a program that prepares students for today and whatever tomorrow brings.

Reference

1. Vocabulary.com (n.d.) *Leader*; www.vocabulary.com/dictionary/leader.

12

Reflect on Your Involvement with the Wider Community

It has been a long journey as you discovered how being *Confident, Committed, Connected, Communicator,* a *Change Agent, Passionate, Purposeful,* a *Planner, Professional, Powerful, Listener, Learner,* and *Leader* work together to make you an Involved School Librarian. Before putting it together as a whole, take time to reflect on the possibilities you developed in your interactions with the wider community outside the school.

For your reflection, use the four domains from AASL's National School Library Standards[1] to identify where you need to go next. Here are some questions and ideas to get you started.

Think

- What actions to reaching parents are simplest for you? How will you increase their connection to and support for the school library program?
- How successfully are you working with the public librarian to best position both libraries to get community support? Which PLNs are giving you the most useful information? Do you need to widen your PLNs? Interact with them more?
- Which business owners and managers are you going to target? Do you already know some of them? Are they the

ones most likely to be open to developing a connection to the library? If not, who are?
- What else has occurred to you about the outside community and its possible affect and support for the library?

Create
- Craft a Vision Statement on who will be with the outside community and what it will produce.
- Develop infographics or other easy to assimilate information on topics of interest to parents.
- Become a more visible presence in the library community to extend the support you get and give from your PLN.
- Create badges, pins, or other visible ways to have business community members show they are library supporters.
- What else can you create to promote the library?

Share
- Use your communication channels with parents for them to share with each other how they have helped in the library, what they liked most about it, and what they learned.
- Write an article or blog post for one of the National School Library Associations.
- Send photos to business community members of a project or author visit showing what their support produced.
- What other ways can you share your successes and acknowledge the support that made them possible?

Grow
- Offer short presentations or webinars to the parent association that will attract attention, bringing more participation in the association and building more support for the library.
- Submit a proposal to present at an upcoming State or National Library Conference.
- Check regularly to identify any new businesses in the community and visit with them.

Putting It All Together

There has been a lot to take in, and it didn't cover everything.

Part I revolved around you. Take time to revisit it and see what more it has to tell you about yourself.

There was some mention of art and music teachers in the school community, but it is larger than that. The school community includes the nurses, the secretaries, the cafeteria workers, and custodial staff. How involved are you with them? What possibilities exist there for the library program?

The outside community has different priority levels. Are you spending enough time there? Too much time? Is there a part that should take a greater amount of your time? Where can you learn more about time management?

With all the new ideas and ways of looking at things, it is wise to once again remember S. R. Ranganathan (www.librarianshipstudies.com/2017/09/five-laws-of-library-science.html). He wrote his Five Laws in 1931. They have been adopted as truisms by librarians ever since. The fifth law, "The Library Is A Growing Organism," is particularly true today as when he wrote it.

It is up to you as a *Leader* to keep your library growing. Make the AASL Vision, "Every School Librarian a *Leader*; Every *Learner* has a School Librarian" a reality.

Reference

1. AASL (2018) *National School Library Standards For Learners, School Librarians, and School Libraries*; ALA Editions: Chicago, Ill.